Do Brown Cows Make Chocolate Milk?

Family Experiences Around Child-Led Learning

By Siva, Aarti, Sarang, and Vivaan Sankrithi

ii

Table of Contents

Acknowledgements

The four of us would like to sincerely thank each and every one of you for supporting our journeys and engaging with our stories. Special thanks to Anya and Asha Wojciechowski for their brilliant illustrations, Adrian Russian for her incredible copyediting, layout work, and testimonial, Ken Lee for his inspiration, Ravi Kakkad for his website marketing help and testimonial, and Maria-Teresa Vicens, Josh Sinanan, Megan Lee, and Conan McLemore for their testimonials. None of this would've been possible without the support of our parents, grandparents, and family. Thank you for providing us with a foundation that we could build upon and refine on our intentional parenting and child-led learning journey.

Testimonials

"I first got to know the Sankrithi family through Siva, who taught me geometry my freshman year of high school. That also happened to be the year Sarang was born, and I remember meeting him when he was just a few weeks old and Siva took a break from his paternity leave to bring him to campus. A few years later, during the summer after my freshman year of college, I spent most of my afternoons babysitting Sarang, while Vivaan napped and Siva ran errands. That summer, I became close with not only Sarang, but every member of the family, as Aarti and Siva were generous enough to let me hang around as long as I wanted even after they got home, and often even let me stay for dinner. Today, I'm living in Italy as a digital nomad, but pretty much every day I take a moment to recognize how fortunate I feel to have spent so much time with the Sankrithis that summer, and to still consider them close friends, whom I make sure to see whenever I'm back in the Pacific Northwest. All four of them are such radiant, thoughtful, and warm people that it's simply impossible to spend time with them and leave without feeling a little more optimistic about the world. That feeling carries over to this book, which I have been fortunate enough to get a preview of while helping the Sankrithis edit it. Even if you don't have kids and/or aren't planning on having them—personally, I'm still undecided there—the philosophies spelled out in this book aren't just applicable to parenting, but to decision-making in the context of any sort of relationship, including the one you have with yourself. The thoughts, experiences, and reflections shared by the Sankrithis do just what Siva used to do for me in geometry class, all those years ago: provide some order and direction, in a world that can feel overwhelming more often than not."

Adrian Russian

*****

"All these years after I met him, I cannot refer to Mr. Sankrithi by his first name. Maybe that's because of my age and cultural background (I was born in Puerto Rico in 1962). Maybe it's because of the respect I have for him. Maybe it's for all those reasons. Mr. Sankrithi taught my daughter math in high school. At his back-to-school-night presentation the first year she was in class with him, I was immediately struck by his genuine passion and obvious gift for teaching young people. At a one-on-one meeting with him later that fall, during a challenging time for our family, I understood firsthand that he truly "walked the talk" of supporting and encouraging his students. Throughout the semester and the rest of the school year, it became apparent to me why he was a legendary teacher at the school. He truly had a gift for connecting with his students, for helping them stay in touch with how rewarding—and yes, fun—math was as they got better at asking the questions that would best help them navigate their way themselves out of difficulties. I am grateful to this day that my daughter's path crossed Mr. Sankrithi's when it did. To this day, he remains a mentor and friend to her, now with the added richness of his wife and their two sons. This is a family that truly and authentically approaches life with delight, enthusiasm, and curiosity for all the wondrous opportunities we are all afforded every day to learn and grow and discover. I look forward to learning and growing and discovering alongside the Sankrithi family."

Maria-Teresa Vicens

*****

"I first met Siva at a scholastic chess event in January 2020. I was wading through a sea of children, trying to help my 4-year old get to his playing room for his first round game. Siva was doing the same with his son and there was an immediate, unspoken, mutual kinship in that moment. What I didn't know at the time was that I had just kicked off a deep adult friendship which is a rare thing, and is even more rare when you realize that the friendship became the seed for an even deeper family-to-family friendship. Over the coming months, our boys met at multiple chess tournaments, became part of a 3-person chess team called the 'Bandar Bhais' (literally, 'Monkey Brothers' in Hindi), and became brotherly buddies through it all.

The Sankrithi's truly are the first family of education in Seattle. Siva's love and natural proclivity for connecting with people is evident from the moment you meet him. Siva is a born educator, who thrives in deep thought, articulation, and the back-and-forth that is the bedrock of teaching. Chess, music, tennis, table tennis, football (both American and global), politics, education, mathematics, travel, and even general pop culture – these are just some of the topics that bring a smile to his face and can lead to a wild conversation where you lose track of time and walk away feeling upbeat about the world and wiser at the same time.

Siva is a prolific writer. I joke that he manages to get his crisp thoughts up on social media (and somehow energizes himself while doing it) before I am even able to get a first draft of my thoughts into my head while also getting exhausted. I was thrilled to hear that Siva, Aarti, Sarang, and Vivaan are putting their thoughts on paper to share them with the world. It is a fun, breezy, and educational read that promises to make you think just enough, while also reminding you not to take things too seriously. This book –just like our interactions with the Sankrithi's – reminds us that no matter where life takes you, it's all about the journey and the little joys along the way."

Ravi Kakkad

*****

"There's no doubt you'll be smiling throughout this book! Siva, Aarti, Sarang, and Vivaan are some of the happiest people I have the pleasure of knowing. Their passion for learning and trying new things is infectious and effervescent. Every time I see the Sankrithi family, there's always a warm and insightful conversation to be had and something new to be learned, whether it's a fun fact about transcontinental airlines or a new chess variant. This book will provide you a unique perspective towards growth and the opportunity for introspection towards your own passions."

Megan Lee

*****

"The Sankrithis – Aarti, Siva, Sarang, and Vivaan – are like a second family to me. From the moment that I set foot in their home each week for chess lessons with their two wonderful boys, Sarang and Vivaan, I'm always greeted by smiling family members and welcomed with a hot cup of chai. I'm lucky if I manage to make it through the chess game unscathed, as both Sarang and Vivaan are two of my most dedicated and fast-improving students. Win or lose, the boys always take a moment to chat and reflect with their opponent after the game and are truly compassionate competitors, something quite unique this day in age. Sarang and Vivaan exhibit a genuine love for learning that is quite uncommon for kids their age. Their parents Aarti and Siva no doubt have played a key role in this, but the boys are also self-directed and motivated from within to pursue their hobbies and passions.

In talking with the Sankrithis, you can tell that they have a wide variety of interests not just limited to chess, music, math, and puzzles. Each of them is working collaboratively to make the world a better place, but in their own way. The Sankrithis spread joy and happiness wherever they go and effortlessly raise the mood of everyone with whom they cross paths. After a visit to the Sankrithi household, you'll leave feeling inspired and energized after spending time with these amazing human beings."

Josh Sinanan

*****

"Siva has been a very good friend for about 20 years and I now have the honor of being Sarang and Vivaan's music teacher. We frequently have very high levels of discussions during their lessons, stemming from their love of music and of learning. Siva and Aarti are both outstanding parents and educators. I can think of no better people to have written this book. The input of all four cannot help but result in an outstanding work on an important facet of education."

Conan McLemore

Introduction

Dear Friends,

Thank you so much for choosing to read our book.
This book has been on our minds a while and writing
it has truly been a labor of love for our family. We're
a quirky family of four of Indian descent living in
Lake Forest Park, Washington, in the United States.
This book will largely be in the collective voice of life
partners Siva #DadLife and Aarti #MomLife, and our
two boys, Sarang, #BigBro, and Vivaan, #LilBro.
This book can be broadly classified as a parenting
book, highlighting child-led learning and intentional
parenting. We hope that you and your loved ones
can read and reflect on our stories together. In every
chapter, all four of us offer our reflections on the
stories shared and we think these reflections will be
great conversation starters.

Our story is a bit unique. Both Siva and Aarti grew up in loving households, finished schooling and college young, married young, and started a family young. In 2016, at the age of 29, Siva retired after a decade of classroom teaching at a prestigious independent school in Seattle to homeschool our boys and do part-time educational consulting. Siva's heart was at home. Aarti's roles have spanned engineering, supply chain, and finance, but being Mom tops that list. Our boys Sarang and Vivaan love chess, music, and travel, and all three will be themes that recur frequently in the book. While we've chosen a path of highly intentional parenting where at least one of us is always home with our boys, our hope is this book will provide useful insights for you, whatever your situation might be.

As you go through the book, you'll notice that every chapter starts with real-life experiences we lived as a family, rooted in a question or statement Sarang or Vivaan made, as well as a thematic idea we feel is a key component of child-led learning: curiosity, planning, exposure, connection, awareness, resilience, privilege, ownership, goals, readiness, pacing, and inspiration. Each chapter finishes with reflections from all of us. While we encourage you to read the book in the order presented, given intentional thematic overlaps, the chapters are all self-contained and can be read independently, and in whatever order you choose. Our hope is that our stories and experiences, and the reflections and ideas that follow, might motivate you to try some things you might not have thought of before. We hope you enjoy our stories, and we can't wait to hear yours.

Love,

The Sankrithi Family

Chapter One
Curiosity

Do Brown Cows Make Chocolate Milk?

O ne day while enjoying a cup of cool chocolate milk, toddler Vivaan asked, "Do brown cows make chocolate milk?" We looked at one another, smiled, and responded with our classic line, "What a great question! What do you think?" What followed was a discussion about mammals, including cows, which produce most of the milk we drink, and how some animals make milk while others don't. He then asked his wizened old brother, six at the time, and Sarang said "I think it's a mixture of plain milk and chocolate." Moments later, the brothers were in the kitchen experimenting with mixing milk and chocolate syrup, and sure enough, they soon had chocolate milk! Although lots of amazing learning had just happened, the thirst for knowledge was far from quenched.

In the days that followed, we visited multiple libraries, checked out numerous books on farming, mammals, and cows, and found various YouTube videos and shows that showed the milk process at work. We visited some local farms to see the process live, and got to really experience what was happening. The boys also learned that there are indeed different types of milk made by different types of cows, and for a little while the boys would only drink Jersey milk from Jersey cows because it was "so much better!" Admittedly we noticed a taste difference as well, but perhaps not quite as pronounced. While all of these experiences didn't fully answer the boys' deeper questions, they did provide them with some context that their initial hypothesis wasn't wildly off base: different cows do produce different types of milk, but perhaps chocolate milk required something more, in bringing in the chocolate component.

A few months later, while visiting their grandparents, we went to a museum and experienced the phenomenal Farm Tech exhibit. The question returned, with a twist. Ok, we've figured out how milk of various varieties gets from the cows (of all colors) to our home, but how does the chocolate? We get all these lovely chocolate bars, hot cocoa, chocolate ice cream, and chocolate milk, but where does the chocolate come from? At this point they moved away from the animal kingdom and started thinking about plants. They were growing all sorts of fruits and vegetables in our garden and saw how we could turn apples, figs, plums, potatoes, carrots, peppers, tomatoes, and more into all sorts of scrumptious things, so maybe chocolate was a fruit or vegetable too?

With a pandemic raging, months of wondering became years, but the answer finally came while visiting a cacao farm on an international trip with grandparents. The previous day we had visited a coconut farm and learned about the varieties of coconut trees, how they grow, what the life of a coconut farmer is like, then picked ripe coconuts, and enjoyed incredibly fresh coconut water. With the interest in farming fully rekindled, we couldn't pass up the opportunity to see the chocolate process at work. After a long day of travelling, we sat down for some ice cream at the little cafe. Vivaan wanted vanilla ice cream and was provided with something light brown in color. "What's that?! Why isn't it white?" The lady who prepared the ice cream smiled and said "This is real vanilla. The vanilla you've had is usually made with extract and doesn't have the same color. See that plant up there? Real vanilla

comes from that. Take a bite. I bet you'll love it."
Sure enough, he did.

Moments after the vanilla revelation, the chocolate questions began percolating again and we were all really excited to go on a tour of the farm to understand how the chocolate process works from start to finish. The hour that followed blew our minds. We saw howler monkeys happily jumping from tree to tree, enjoying fruit and each other's company, and plants we'd never get to see back home. Our guide stopped us at one particular plant and the boys were quick to inquire as to what those yellow-orange fruit they'd never seen before were. She went on to explain that that is the Theobroma plant and those fruit are cacao! Wait, wait, wait. Epiphanous moment approaching! Cacao sounds like cocoa and cocoa is chocolate! That's where chocolate comes from?! No way! She asked the boys if they wanted to pick one and they eagerly did, and after cutting it open, what they saw was shocking... There were little things that looked like beans covered in a white goo of some sort. We each plucked a little gooey bean out and gave it a taste.

The outside was a very interesting texture and the inside almost tasted like chocolate! Some crunchy, bitter, strange fruit chocolate.

We went on to witness the fermenting process, drying process, roasting process, and more, and learn how ancient cultures did this work manually for many centuries. It was eye opening for the kids to see such an intricate process happening without any technology. After winnowing and using a grindstone to crush the cocoa beans, the sweet smell of chocolate filled the room. The boys were completely transfixed and eager to eat some. To their surprise what they tasted was quite bitter, though we rather enjoyed it. What happened? We all just had our eyes opened and minds blown and after all that effort experiencing the chocolate process, we have just a tiny bit of bitter brown goo? That's not what we get at home! At that moment, Sarang, now nine, figured it out. Hold on, maybe this is 100% dark chocolate! We need to add sugar! Sure enough, the next step in our chocolate game was adding some sugar, vanilla, and honey to our chocolate and mixing it in well. The smell and taste of the chocolate they love was everywhere! Yes! They'd done it! Even then, they realized, much like milk, the variations in chocolate are huge. This didn't taste at all like the chocolate bars back home or the syrup they put in their chocolate milk. It was different, but it was awesome.

In the days that followed, as we continued exploring on our trip, the conversations and reflections we had with the boys were remarkable. Their appreciation for people had grown. Their appreciation for hard work had grown. Their wonder at how much goes into creating something we completely take for granted was at an all-time high. Their curiosity about processes behind the goods they get so easily at home was piqued. So sugar comes from those sugar canes we see on the side of the road here. Honey comes from bees. Chocolate comes from cocoa beans which come from a cacao pod which comes from the Theobroma plant. Milk comes from cows. Then it all gets combined and packaged and somehow gets to a grocery store where we can buy it and enjoy it? Oh man. Time to introduce them to supply chains!

Time. Your time. While we acknowledge that spending time with your kids in the amounts you want can be challenging given work schedules and social calendars and what not, the reality is that if you don't take the time to foster their curiosity and student-led learning, even if it's just a little every day, or every week, or whatever you can do, their curiosity might decline, as it has for so many, and that's a tragedy. You may not have time to answer every question they ask (and we know they ask a LOT) but try not to dismiss them. Put it back on them. What do you think? Check out this book. Check out this website. Check out this video online. Whatever it might be. Ask your sibling. Ask your friend. You have the time for that. Trust us, it'll be worth your while. The child who loves learning and is innately curious will grow in ways you might never expect and the results are truly miraculous.

Another fascinating element to student-led-learning is the unexpected takeaways and the willingness to go where the learning takes you. You may start with one question and end up answering a hundred others. We live in such a prescribed world governed by schedules, charts, benchmarks, and checklists to "help" parents make sure their children are learning and developing at an age-appropriate level, that we forget to let them be children. We forget to let them run with that youthful aplomb and explore, get messy, ask questions, dig deeper, and find answers to questions we may never have even thought of. They have a lifetime ahead of them when they can live a prescribed life (should they choose to do so). Why prematurely curb that youthful zeal with overly structured adult prescription? As for checking those boxes, isn't it incredible that once they do solve whatever curiosity they're exploring, they become even more curious about what comes next? That's the beauty of childhood and child-led learning!

There are several critical takeaways for us as parents, educators, and really anyone engaging with kids. Kids are innately curious. Kids love to learn. Kids ask a lot of questions and while we can easily be dismissive or respond with a simple yes or no, perhaps we should instead turn it back around and let them explore. Let them take the lead. Let their ideas percolate. Let them hypothesize. Let them experiment. Let them ideate. We can ask interesting questions to help encourage and facilitate their learning and provide them with resources and experiences that might help them. In the education world, we call this the Socratic method and experiential education. We call this way of learning student-led-learning or student-centered-learning. How did it start in our story above? It was a very natural question from a curious toddler that we could've easily dismissed.

Sarang and Vivaan's Reflections

It was so fun making chocolate but it was hard work and took some strong arms! It's such a treat drinking chocolate milk now that we know all the work that goes into it! We were a little nervous to try farming but we did it and it's great! Maybe one day we'll be farmers and chefs and we can run a restaurant serving food only we grow! We think we'll grow wheat to make flour for bread and pasta, lots of fruits and vegetables so we can make sandwiches, have cows so we can get milk and make cheese, sugar cane so we can sweeten our dishes, and maybe some chocolate for dessert!

<u>Chapter Two</u>
Planning

Can I Ride the Bison?

K ids have ideas. Lots and lots of ideas. As parents, it is often tricky to strike the right balance between encouragement of these ideas, and realism about the possibility of executing them. The keys have been helping the boys learn how to gameplan, anticipate which ideas might work, be open to experimentation and failure, and enjoy the process of hard work and iteration. Now, can you really teach a toddler planning? Turns out you can. Our family loves food, and since the boys were very little, both loved helping us in the kitchen. "Can we be your pizza sous chefs?" "Can we bake cookies?" "Can we make lemonade?" You name it, we tried it. That said, we never told them what to do. Instead, we had them figure out their own plan. Oh, you want to make pizza? What do you think you need? Flour. Ok. Sauce. Cool. Cheese. Alright. Basil. Nice. Etc. We'd watch videos, read recipes, experiment—a lot—and have tons of fun in the process.

Sometimes, their plan felt a little too ambitious for that evening, and that was ok. Perhaps it could be punted to another time. A great example is when

Vivaan wanted to make doughnuts during the holidays. He did his research, figured out was what needed, and came up with a plan. But sometimes plans have hitches. We went to buy a doughnut pan and the stores were all out. Then he saw a pan with molds for snowmen, gingerbread men, and trees, and asked "Can we make those doughnuts?" Of course we turned the question back on him, and once he came to terms with the fact that the torus shape isn't really what makes a doughnut taste so yummy, he excitedly said "Let's do it!" The rest is history. Holiday season 2022: this kid makes the best doughnuts we ever tasted, in some wild non-doughnut-shaped shapes!

While the kitchen is one of the most amazing places to teach about planning and experimentation, travel has been another incredible opportunity for our boys to practice these skills. In the middle of 2022, Vivaan was researching animals—one of his favorite pastimes—and was absolutely fascinated by bison. They were enormous. They were right here in the USA. Naturally the excited four-year-old asked "Can

I ride the bison?" While theoretically possible, we felt that discretion, given the vast size discrepancy and wild nature of most bison, was warranted. So, we diverted a little bit and asked him to research where he could find bison, and see if he could plan a trip around going to see them. Enter Sarang, the then eight-year-old trip planner extraordinaire.

In the weeks that followed, the boys worked together to plan out an incredible trip that neither of us could've possibly come up with ourselves. Firstly, bison. Where could they see bison that wasn't super full of people? North Dakota. Theodore Roosevelt National Park. Ok. How to get there? Fly? Drive? Hmmm… They began researching things around North Dakota. They found the Garden of a Thousand Buddhas in Arlee, Montana. We'd never heard of it, but it sounded pretty sweet! They found the Mobius Discovery Center in Spokane, WA. They found Mall of America and Nickelodeon Universe in Minnesota. It was all starting to come together. Road trip?! Road trip! Let's see grandparents in Illinois too! At this point in their planning process, they brought us in, as we are the fiscal backers of many of their adventures, not to mention the transportation as they do not yet drive cars, though they may drive the ideas.

We told them when this trip could work with our schedules, then had them think about how many hours a day they wanted to be in the car, how many attractions they wanted to see, any friends or family they might like to meet along the way, etc. What followed was remarkable. Sarang may well become a travel agent one day. No more than six hours a day in the car, because that's more than enough for Vivaan. Jerry-rigged Nintendo Switch setup in the backseat for at least an hour a day to break up some of the journey. Where to get gas. Which hotels to stay at. Which restaurants we might like. Which friends we could see. The boys planned everything. They also insisted that they travel blog the entire journey, so they had access to our phones for pictures and our Facebook pages for one post a day reflecting on what they saw/did. This has since become a tradition on all our trips, one we'd highly recommend you try with your own kiddos.

While we could write for days about this particular road trip, we'll just share a few highlights and takeaways. After a wonderful time at the Mobius museum in Spokane, the boys found a tent where volunteers were offering bottles of water for anyone walking by. They were touched. They offered to pay, but the friends refused saying this is their way of giving back, by helping the community beat the heat. In Montana, we met some of our friends, and visited the Buddha Garden. It was incredible. There were chants written in several languages, including Japanese and Sanskrit, both languages the boys had been studying. No tech, crisp mountain air, and a thousand spectacular statues nestled in the foothills. Truly unforgettable.

When we reached the Theodore Roosevelt National Park, we were welcomed by a few prairie dogs posing for us, giving us a namaste of sorts, and golden eagles circling above. As we drove through the park, getting further and further away from civilization and any other cars, we saw wild horses, pronghorn deer, and gophers enjoying their natural habitat. Not losing hope of seeing a bison, we kept going, deeper and deeper into the park. About ninety minutes into our exploration, which was already life-changing in so many ways, a truly unbelievable thing happened. At this point there were no other cars on the road. Just us. And nature. Vivaan yells from the backseat: "Dad, stop!"

We stopped. About ten feet in front of the car, on the other side of the street, we saw him. A gigantic, 2000 pound (at least), male bison, who seemed to wink at us, or at the very least acknowledge our presence and thank us for stopping. Was this really happening?! Sarang was freaking out a little bit, wondering if we were going to die, and Vivaan was once again wondering if he could ride our new friend. What a fun little microcosm of their personalities! This gargantuan bison then happily walked across the road in front of us and down to the water on the other side of the street to grab a drink. We fortunately had the wherewithal to whip out a phone and videotape the event for future enjoyment, and in that moment, our four-year-old, who asked us to ride a bison and planned an epic road trip with his brother, said: "My dream came true!"

The rest of the trip was lovely. They got their Nintendo time. They visited some arcades. We met lots of friends. We went to Nickelodeon Universe. We even, through their travel blogging, realized some dear friends, who'd moved to the East coast years before, were road-tripping West as we road-tripped East, and we met up for lunch in the middle of Wisconsin! We then had a wonderful time with their grandparents. Amazing as the entire trip was, when they're asked about the journey in a decade, or perhaps when they're telling the story to their kids or grandkids down the line, you know they're going to talk about that bison. Not only the event itself, of seeing that monumental creature crossing right in front of our car, but the fact that they planned the trip themselves, and that it all started with a simple question from a little boy hoping to ride a bison.

What's the Cost?

The adults need to be willing to cede some control to their children, which can be hard. The adults also need to have some trust in their kids. Yes, we need to be there to offer reason and provide parameters, to prevent infeasible plans from happening. That said, we can give just basic scaffolding and guidance, and from there let the kids take ownership of their ideas, and authentically contribute to the plans with their creative ingenuity. The other cost is time. It's easy to plan a trip now with websites that can do everything for you, not to mention travel agents. It takes time to let your kids take the lead, ideate, and gradually converge upon a gameplan. That said, trust us when we say, it'll be family time well spent.

What jumps out at us is the importance of planning in children's lives. Yes, we parents plan. Sometimes too much. Sometimes too little. We're not judging. But whether you're more of a go with the flow parent, a super structured one, or anywhere in between, planning is a skill kids need to learn, and truth be told, it's never too early. Letting kids take ownership of the planning process in relatively safe, controlled environments like the kitchen or when making travel itineraries, so that they can try, fail, ideate, and iterate with you there to loosely vet their process and decisions, makes a world of difference to them. They feel like they're contributing to their family in meaningful ways, which they are. They're also developing critical thinking and deeper planning skills that will serve them so well as they grow throughout their childhood, adolescence, and eventually adulthood.

Another critical reason to let children plan is to introduce parameters and constraints in thoughtful ways. Let them lead and run with their imaginations.

But when they want to stick their hands in the 400-degree oven to get the donuts, you of course introduce the gloves, or tell them they can do that in a few years. When they want to stay at fancy hotels during every stop of the journey, maybe introduce a budget. When they want to drive from Seattle to Chicago in a day, introduce some time parameters and have them think about sleep. Helping kids consider roadblocks and thoughtfully navigate around them is one of the greatest superpowers we have as parents.

Vivaan's Reflection

If you want to ride a bison, you need to be careful. It could really hurt you. I wanted to ride a bison but instead I planned a trip to see them in real life and we did! Maybe I'll ride a horse. Those seem safer. Now I cook more than my brother. It's very fun and a good way to try new things. It really doesn't matter what ingredients you put in, you can try anything, but some things taste better than others and often following recipes help the food taste yummier. Then again, if you don't have the correct leaf, just use another leaf, and you should be good to go!

Sarang's Reflection

I love planning trips. So far, I've planned about five family vacations. First, I start with maps and figure out how long it takes to go from place to place. Then I research on TripAdvisor and with AAA books, and by talking with family and friends, to find attractions for us to go see. Once I have a sense of where all we'll go and time constraints day by day, I search for hotels where we can spend each night. They need to be comfortable, affordable, and not too far out of the way. Hopefully they have a good breakfast too! We're vegetarian and we love food so I also research restaurants. Some places are not as vegetarian-friendly as others. I also check several airlines when we're flying to find good prices and timing that works out for our sleep schedules. When we're driving, I look for gas stations, taking into account the gas mileage for our cars. Thinking about where to go in the future, we often have family conversations where we each rank our dream destinations locally, nationally, and internationally, and try to find common ground. When we do pick places internationally, I like to research culture and

language and at least learn some basic
conversational words and phrases to help there.
Maybe I could be a travel agent some day!

<u>Chapter Three</u>
Exposure

*Can We Go to Music Man
Stan's Music Shop?*

Even before becoming parents, music always played a major role in our lives. Aarti grew up singing in the South Indian Carnatic Classical vocal tradition, then learned Western choral music, acapella vocals, and piano, and now sings in the North Indian Hindustani Classical vocal tradition. Siva grew up with Western choral music and flute, and is now part of a flute choir, playing piccolo, concert flute, alto flute, and bass flute. We guessed music might play a part in our kiddos' lives, but didn't really know when or how.

For those who have watched *Daniel Tiger's Neighborhood* on PBS Kids, you've probably heard of Music Man Stan's Music Shop, an incredible place of pure joy, filled with music of all kinds. We watch shows with our kids, and actively engage with those shows to give us a common language we can use in other facets of our lives. While toddler Sarang had some musical proclivities from watching us do our things, he didn't really start his own journey until he asked us "Can we go to Music Man Stan's Music Shop?"

What followed was a deep dive into every sort of music. We decided that, though we adults converged on certain musical traditions and instruments, the key for our kids would be to expose them to as much music as possible, and let them choose what they liked themselves. We went to some music stores, and Sarang's eyes lit up around the piano, drums, and ukulele, not to mention the melodica, a curious piano-like instrument you blow air into to generate sound. Awesome, let's try them all! We were especially thrilled to see piano on his list of interesting instruments, given the numerous benefits of learning melodies, harmonies, and composition within that medium, not to mention deeper music theory down the line. We were also excited for drums, as the benefits of rhythm permeate all music. Of course, all instruments require keen hand-eye coordination and, as learning progresses, an ability to think deeply about incorporating emotion, musicality, and more. Curiously, Vivaan converged on similar instruments as a toddler, although he did add the awesomely percussive boom whackers to the mix, which incorporate rhythm and melody simultaneously, as well as harmonica.

We found Sarang a teacher, an old friend of Siva's from his University of Washington music days, to help him learn music theory, composition, piano, and drums. His teacher harnessed Sarang's passion for music by initially focusing more on breadth than depth, then diving deep when Sarang was ready, simultaneously challenging Sarang and maximizing his enthusiasm. Recognizing his penchant for patterns, his teacher challenged Sarang to write a piece that was a palindrome, meaning it reads the same backwards and forwards. It took time, iteration, and lots of experimentation but he did it! Scored for flute (so Dad could play), piano (so Mom could play), and drums (so he could play), his piece was brilliant, and even premiered remotely via video at a concert for charity during Covid!

As time progressed, Sarang joined a Disco band, leading the group from the drumkit. With piano, he focused more on the Western Classical tradition, and when he began playing the likes of Chopin and Debussy as an eight-year-old, piano became a brilliant way for him to not only grow his musicality, but also express his emotions, which is often challenging for us hyperrational folk. At the end of the day, whatever challenges our kids face in life, finding opportunities for them to share their feelings, in ways they are comfortable doing so, is critical. Music has provided our boys with such an emotive outlet, as it has done so beautifully for us.

We also made it a point to have music around us constantly. Sure, we already loved music and listened often. But when we recognized Sarang's love for music, we made sure we were thoughtful about his exposure to music, focusing on breadth and helping him develop his own stylistic preferences, even if they differed our own, a practice we've continued with Vivaan. We intentionally choose songs representative of different genres, and look at various covers to help them understand both similarities and differences in multiple interpretations of the same song.

We used to regularly play a music guessing game, where one of us would be the DJ and the others would guess the title and artist(s) on the track as quickly as possible. Sarang soon became the best, naming the tunes at an incredible rate, even if he'd only heard them once before. For example, one day as we were driving to chorus, the song "Africa" came on the radio. Sarang had likely heard it once or twice. Aarti was quick on the draw, and said "Africa" by Toto in under a second after hearing the opening chords. Within another second, however, Sarang calmly said "No Mom. This is 'Africa' by Weezer. It's one and a half steps up."

A phenomenal aspect of musical exposure has been connecting Sarang to his cultural roots and motherland, India. Siva may have been born and raised in the USA, but Aarti grew up in India. Around seven, Sarang began studying Carnatic vocal music. His teacher, also his aunt, is incredible as not only a professional Western and Indian singer but, like him, a person of Indian origin born and raised in the USA. For Sarang, music has connected him with both his grandparents and his great-grandparents. One of his great-grandmothers loves piano, and watching an under ten-year-old and his over 90-year-old great-grandma playing Bach and Beethoven together is something else.

As for the Carnatic music, it's a common music language shared by all who have learned it, and watching friends and family of all ages living all over the world come together through music is beautiful to witness. It's remarkable how everyone who learns Carnatic music follows a consistent pedagogical process and can come together in song and appreciate all the subtle intricacies that are presented by performers. In our cultural tradition, there's a monthlong celebration of music called Margazhi Utsavam. For many people, from all axes of our family, especially Siva's grandfather, this celebration is an opportunity to reflect, enjoy music, and connect with each other. In late 2022, Sarang had the honor of being invited to perform during this month. He practiced hard and sang well, and more importantly was able to thoughtfully reflect on his experience bonding with so many family members through this common language of music.

With a music-loving Mom, Dad, and brother, Vivaan was exposed to everything very young, and had a keen ear for many forms of music even as a toddler. At age three, he started learning drums and piano from the same creative music teacher as Sarang. The pace was slow and steady, and fit his readiness level beautifully. The lesson started as five minutes before Sarang's. Then it became ten. Then fifteen. You get the idea.

As Covid restrictions started loosening and Vivaan got a bit older, more patient, and more confident, he expressed interest in joining Sarang's disco band and gospel choir. Remarkably, both the leaders of those groups had the vision to be totally amenable to letting him join, though he was just four. Note here too the interest came from him. He knew the music conceptually and could theoretically play it for a while too. That said, practically, as a young four-year-old, he wasn't ready for the rigors of hour-long rehearsals, repeated practice, sitting still, focusing, and performing with kids of all ages (both groups feature teenagers as well as children).

Sometime in his late fours, everything clicked. He told us: "Dad and Mom, When I turn five, I'm going to be ready for ALL the activities." While somewhat hyperbolic, it also had some truth. More than anything, he'd found his voice. He'd fully found his confidence. Sure he still sounded like a toddler, albeit a slightly deeper-voiced one. Sure he wasn't super comfortable yet reading music and lyrics with big words. That said, because he'd been exposed to so much music growing up, and already experienced so many rehearsals from the sideline as Sarang's brother, engaging with the older kids as a buddy and their de facto little bro, he was ready, and the teachers in both the disco band and gospel choir saw it.

At his second disco rehearsal, comfortably the youngest of ten in the band, he began to find his groove. He followed the lead singers beautifully, joined in on the choruses, and by the end of rehearsal was happily singing along full voiced. Two remarkable things happened that day. First, mid-rehearsal as Sarang saw and heard Vivaan singing the choruses, he looked at him from his drum kit, the brothers locked eyes, and Sarang gave Vivaan a huge thumbs up and said, "Yes Vivi. You got this. Good job." It was lovely. There was no possessiveness. There was no "This is my band" sentiment. It was pure joy and love and pride in seeing his little brother step up and join the fun. The second remarkable thing happened on the way home. From his booster seat, Vivi asked us if we could listen to "Good Times" and "I Will Survive" more at home, so he could sing along and practice his lyrics and melodies. He was locked in. He had been exposed to music he really enjoyed, given the opportunity to engage with it, and now wanted to put in the work to get better. That's what it's all about.

What's the Cost?

Well, literally speaking, money. Music lessons cost money. Buying an instrument costs money. That said, there are lots of opportunities out there to explore music at little cost, or even for free. Many choirs and musical groups also offer scholarship programs for those struggling to pay. Other groups offer free "Bring A Friend" days, where you can sit in on a class and see if it's something your child would enjoy. School and after school programs are also a great way for kids to try different activities, even things they haven't seen you do before. The other potential cost here, which we often hear from parents, is "You got your kid a drum set? How can you deal with the noise?" Look. Kids love practicing music. That's the honest truth. What they don't like is being told they're bad and that they need to keep it down. So don't do that! Put in subtly-disguised ear plugs if you must, but just roll with it. Let them explore. Let them have fun. Let them learn. Trust us, you'll look back on those early days, where the sounds feel a lot more like noise than music, fondly.

Music is powerful as a universal language and a connector between people from all walks of life, of all ages, and with all different backgrounds. Exposing kids to a wide range of music, free from our own biases, makes a world of difference to helping them find their own path. The perceived correlation between age and ability is questionable at best. Assessing readiness is challenging, so let them run with what they're into (within reason). More broadly, exposure is key to helping kids find themselves. We as parents can be thoughtful about which of our interests we want to expose our kids to and when, but at the same time, we want to consciously expose them to varied experiences that may differ from our own, to let them find their own voice and passions. It merits mention too that while music was the focus of this chapter, and is and will hopefully continue to be an integral part of our lives, you could easily substitute music with art, sports, reading, writing, coding, or whatever you want. The general takeaway is the same: broader exposure empowers kids to find their passions. When a kid finds a genuine passion, they learn better and they enjoy their learning more, as they want to dive deep into it and put in the work to grow their understanding.

Vivaan's Reflection

Most little kids don't do too many activities but I love them, and I have teachers who let me try. I love music. I love singing. I love piano. I love drums. I love harmonica. I love ukulele. I love singing songs. I love making my own songs. Music makes me feel happy. I've also made friends from music. Sometimes when I don't know what to sing, I listen to the others in the group and listen and learn from them.

Sarang's Reflection

I started actively learning music when I was three or four years old. Music is a major part of my life and is overall my favorite activity. It has really helped me with my hand-eye coordination, and given me fast fingers that help in video games. Through a shared love of music, I've also made many friends. One of the challenges for me is to keep calm. Music helps me do that. Sometimes when I'm mad or sad or not feeling too great, I play piano and express my emotions through the music. It's very helpful. I also have perfect pitch. It's one of my superpowers. It's also kind of a curse. I can't go to birthday parties and hear kids singing happy birthday because it's so out of tune and actually hurts my ears. Actually just going about day-to-day life, so many things are out of tune and as I've grown up, I've learned to tune them out. I'm Indian-American. Learning Indian music has helped me a lot with connecting with my Indian heritage. It's so fun to sing and play with my family and friends of all ages, including my great-grandmothers.

Chapter Four
Connection

If I Become Fluent in Japanese Can We Visit Tokyo?

The ability to communicate and engage with one another is vital. Language development helps. Some say it needs to happen from birth. Others say as toddlers. Others say as youth. Others say anytime. Whatever the case may be, as a family with diverse friend circles, that also likes to travel and engage with new experiences wherever we go, language plays a major role in how we bring up our boys. As a toddler, Sarang was quite introverted and mostly shared his thoughts with only those of us whom he was closest to. When Vivaan arrived, that changed, and Sarang really came out of his shell, largely motivated by his little brother.

Let's back up. Siva grew in the United States, monolingual in English, and though he could understand our mother tongue of Tamil, he never grew comfortable speaking it. As he grew up, he learned Spanish and is reasonably fluent now, which has proven most useful over the years. Aarti grew up in India, multilingual in English and Tamil, and today can get by in Hindi, and speak Spanish as well. With two little boys eager to learn languages, we had some choices to make. Would we raise them bilingually from day one? What would those languages be? Would we stick with English? Ultimately, as with most of our parenting decisions, we let them take the lead and went with where their interests took them. What developed was remarkable.

Both our boys were early talkers. They loved language: exploring it, experimenting with it, and communicating in all forms. As toddlers, they heard lots of Tamil, Hindi, and Spanish from various places, and began asking questions about what this or that meant. They learned a little here and there. Then one day we were at the playground playing with a group of students from a school for the hard of hearing. There they witnessed sign language for the first time. In the week that followed, they insisted on learning some ASL (American Sign Language), so they memorized all the signs for letters and some basic phrases.

At a chess tournament when he was seven, Sarang made a friend who had just come to the US from Mongolia. Without missing a beat, he taught himself several basic Mongolian phrases and pieces of chess terminology, and set up a weekly Zoom call to not only practice language with his new buddy but play some great chess, a tradition that continues today. I remember in the first few weeks, they would try to play hand and brain chess with one other, where one says the name of the piece and the other moves that piece. Sarang would say the names of the pieces in Mongolian and his friend would move. His friend would say the names of the pieces in English and Sarang would move. It was beautiful.

Then came a trip to Belize and Mexico. Keen on being able to communicate with those who might not be proficient in English, the boys were more focused on fluency, and taught themselves some more Spanish and began practicing conversations with us. Thematically, we realized that when there's a reason to learn a language—an authentic reason that the kids see—their retention and eagerness to learn, not to mention their work ethic, all increase tremendously.

The boys' desire to learn Japanese had been building a while. They love Mario Kart, Super Mario, and all other things Mario related. Pokémon is another source of joy for them. There was also a day when they were watching a YouTube video where another kid began learning Japanese. Whatever the source, learning Japanese became a passion, especially for Sarang. He began studying every day, many days for several hours, poring over hiragana, katakana and kanji (different letter systems), and practicing his reading, writing, and speaking. He'd go to the local Asian market and read all the boxes and labels. He learned that the lady at the local coffee shop spoke Japanese and began ordering everything in Japanese. He learned that his tennis coach spoke Japanese and began speaking in Japanese there too. He even wrote letters in Japanese, offering greetings and thanks to friends who spoke. We weren't sure whether this was a "phase" or not, but whatever the case may be, we wanted to empower it. He began doing targeted learning modules online, and his proficiency increased. One day he asked us: "If I become fluent in Japanese, can we visit Tokyo?"

He may not be fluent yet, but he's getting there, and you can guess that we'll absolutely take him to Tokyo when he is. In fact, he's already begun researching all the spots he wants to see in Tokyo and around Japan. He's researched the culture there and is truly fascinated by some of the marked differences between American culture, Indian culture, and Japanese culture, as well as some of the intersections. He's teaching Vivaan as well, and now they can have their coded bro conversations that neither of us can understand! That's a rather powerful motivator too.

It has always intrigued us how here in the U.S., we're so checklist driven. Can they say this many words at this age? Can they write their name? Can they do this? Can they say that? Can they ride a three-wheeler? We've always had the mindset that they'll learn at their own pace and have different passions come and go. If we can empower these passions when they arise, we're doing a pretty good job.

Learning English is another grand adventure. Both boys have great English. It's their first and primary language. Reading, writing, speaking, and storytelling all happen daily in our house as we homeschool. It may not be super structured, but significant learning is happening. You may have wondered how a nine- and four-year-old have been able to be co-authors on this book. Practice. Do we insist they write about specific themes, as is often the case in more conventional educational settings? No. We let them roll with their passions and just provide the scaffolding for them to thrive.

For example, as Sarang was really finding his identity and voice, along with his proclivity towards data and analysis, he started a political podcast, writing a script for each episode, making a PowerPoint, and practicing his speaking. Or, one summer with a buddy, he wrote a three-part fiction graphic novel about their adventures, intertwining reality with creative elements from their active imaginations. Journaling and reflective writing soon followed, as a lovely way to process and synthesize new experiences and lessons learned. Travel blogs, videogame essays, reflections on doctor appointments, reflections on chess tournaments, and even published pieces in magazines happened next.

As for reading, we read lots of books, in the usual progression from picture books to short stories where the kids could read along with us, identifying words they knew and eventually using phonetics to sound it all out independently. The great comprehension epiphanies came when we read the *Harry Potter* series as a family. The boys were transfixed. It was a deep dive into a new world embedded in our world, with elements of reality intertwined with thrilling fictional elements. The boys pushed each other by asking thoughtful, challenging questions of one another. They tested their reading comprehension, ability to extrapolate and anticipate what might come next. Aarti and Siva were Potterheads in our teenage years, enjoying new book releases and the movies as they came out. Incredible storytelling aside, we also told them that they could only watch each movie once they finished each book. This journey took several months, but it was phenomenal. Every day we had trivia games, and discussions about not only the denotations we witnessed in our readings that day, but also the deeper connotations and messaging.

As a homeschooling family in Washington State, we test annually, and unsurprisingly, after this experience together, Sarang's performance on the reading comprehension, vocabulary, and verbal reasoning rose significantly. Speaking of said performance, it merits mention that both boys are excelling well beyond their age-based grade-level, and empowering child-led learning as parents via immersive experiences and connections is a major reason behind that.

What's the Cost?

Look. We get that we're in a unique situation centered around our kids and being able to provide them a great deal of our time, as well as immersive experiences that foster their learning and growth. You may not have that kind of time. That's ok. You can supplement what they're learning in school with fun, immersive opportunities from time to time, and offer them opportunities to connect to those who may have differing interests or perspectives than your own. Maybe it's a family visit to the county fair. Maybe it's a road trip. Maybe it's having a dinner with a neighbor who is from a different culture. Maybe it's spending time with a grandparent learning a traditional recipe. Whatever it is, try to be intentional about it. Have fun. Take pictures. Enjoy. Ask some leading questions. Offer time for reflection. Let them journal or blog. It'll make a world of difference to their retention and ability to synthesize those experiences and connect them to others, past, present, and future.

Our biggest takeaways are the power of immersive learning, running with children's interests, and the power of connecting with people, whether it's in learning a new language, learning English, or learning to read. When the interest is there, so is the drive, work ethic, passion, and love of learning. That interest may be created by friendship, inspiration, or really any form of connection. When it's there, it's awesome to leverage. Siva first learned about the Colorado College model of immersive learning while teaching high school and chatting with some students exploring the idea. This immersive learning model is broadly that students would take one course at a time, for a shorter duration. By deeply immersing themselves in the course, their retention, love of learning, desire to continue, and mastery would increase. It sounded amazing, and he wondered what it would look like applied to younger kids. Working with kids of all ages now in his private consulting work, as well as experiential education organizations around the world, Siva has found that this immersive learning model is brilliant for people of any age. It features a little bit of everything, with deep dives into existing passions, and proves tremendously fruitful for thoughtful learning, retention, and even performance, though that might not be our primary focus. Interestingly enough, the same model can be applied even in a corporate environment. Aarti regularly uses the same approach to help extend the skills of the teams she leads – and it all starts with making a connection, understanding what someone is interested in, and supporting them with resources and scaffolding to help drive their learning process.

Learning languages is hard but super useful. We don't know what we'll become when we grow up but we know that by speaking lots of languages, we can make great connections, visit lots of places, talk to lots of people, and make many friends. Our goal is to be fluent in English, Mandarin, Hindi, Spanish, French, and Arabic, in addition to Japanese and Tamil, because with those first six, you can communicate in over half the world! We're hopeful that by learning languages, we can continue being a team and work together to make the world a better place.

Chapter Five
Awareness

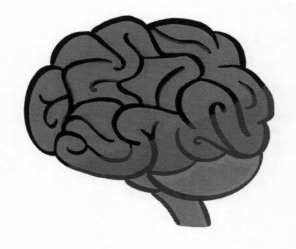

My Prefrontal Cortex Is Developing and Reacting!

F eelings and emotions are challenging for all of us to navigate. Bring in the unique physical and mental obstacles of infancy, toddlerhood, and early childhood, and that challenge often seems overwhelming. In his fours, Sarang was fascinated by the human brain, and sought to understand it a little better. Naturally we provided him resources to do so, and worked to educate ourselves so we could help him. One day, he was having some feelings leading up to his soccer practice, and was composing himself as he walked out onto the field. When his coach noticed and asked what the matter was, he casually responded, "My prefrontal cortex is developing and reacting." Shocked, his coach looked up at me, and then proceeded to laugh that sort of what-did-I-just-hear-and-how-is-this-happening sort of laugh. That laughter immediately snapped the kid out of his funk, and he had a wonderful practice.

A rather funny conversation between Siva and Sarang followed shortly after:

Siva: "If you could solve any problem, what would it be?"

Sarang: "All of them!"

Ok first of all, what a classic, brilliant, amazing, four-year-old response. Nothing can stand in my way!

Siva: "Wow! How will you solve all of them?"

Sarang: "With my hammer and my brain."

Whoa, interesting. This is taking a rather curious turn.

Siva: "Which is more important?"

Sarang: "Both."

Siva: "Oh, ok. What's the process?"

Without missing a beat, the four-year-old jumps in with one of the most Sarang responses ever.

Sarang: "When I see the problem, my prefrontal cortex will react. My cerebral cortex will think and make a plan. My motor cortex will then make me hammer."

Doesn't get much better than that. Details can be figured out later.

Coming back to emotional management, it's especially hard when one is hyperrational, ultra-literal, profoundly gifted, or whatever you wish to call the superpowers or perceived impediments many of us possess. The list could certainly be extended to include any neurodivergent trait, or really anything we learn about ourselves while growing up that might make us feel different from those around us. That realization of difference is a challenge every human being faces at some point or another in their lives.

One morning, both boys were feeling some big feelings. At the time, Sarang was eight and Vivaan was four. We have lots of ways to navigate our emotions, some more traditional than others, but on this particular morning, we decided to do things a little differently. We created a game. A beautiful, emotive, musical game.

At the time, Sarang was learning Beethoven's "Moonlight Sonata" on the piano. We challenged him to showcase a different emotion with each new melodic phrase or repetition of the same melodic idea. Then it was on Vivaan and us to guess the emotions, in order, when the piece concluded. Next, Vivaan, who was learning paradiddles on the drums, had the same challenge: drum a series of emotions using paradiddle rhythms, and we and Sarang would guess the emotions. It was challenging, and it was AMAZING. They explored happiness, sadness, anger, fear, surprise, determination, pride, sleepiness, excitement, and confidence, to name a few. When one wasn't guessed correctly, they worked to re-express the emotion to help us get it. To this day, this game continues to prove amazing not only for managing emotions, but for bringing out musicality as well! We encourage you to give it a go yourselves. Don't have instruments? No problem. Grab a couple of spoons and hit a table, or clap with different rhythms, speeds, and volumes, trying to articulate different emotions using only those "instruments." Or sing a simple tune in different ways to convey different emotions. It's simultaneously challenging, fun, and thought-provoking, not to mention cathartic.

Another major challenge we have to navigate as parents is when other kids behave in ways that are completely incongruous with how we're raising our kids, often causing emotional harm. We all know it happens, whether at activities, or school, or really anywhere. When feelings get hurt, tempers may flare in the moment, and the reaction is often delayed until they come home and vent to you. How we react to, and help them learn from, these moments of adversity is critical, and once again the key is awareness.

For a long time, Sarang got super on edge when people would make noises when they weren't supposed to, especially at chess tournaments. He would melt down after his game and blame his performance on the noise, which shouldn't have been there, but often is, especially with little kids. We had numerous conversations about actions he could take to work on this, though the fault was not his. He could ask them politely to stop tapping their pencil incessantly, or stop talking about the position as it's distracting, not to mention against the rules. He could call a tournament director to help enforce said rules. That said, those are practical things that may or may not work in the moment. Regardless of whether the "what you're supposed to do in these moments" boilerplate works, finding personal ways to move on and stay the course is important. Broadly speaking, others are going to do what others are going to do, and it is your choice how to react. We practiced playing chess at home with music. We practiced playing chess at home with little brother having free reign to distract at will. We practiced with crazy Dad making random hoots and hollers here and there so when Sarang next faced the challenge come tournament time, and even if the practical steps failed, he'd be ok.

At camps and such, other kids would get physical, so we had discussions about setting boundaries, being very clear and confident in saying no, and expressing their disinterest in physical play, as well as about actionable steps to stop it like talking to the coach or teacher. When negative things were said, once again we discussed both practical and theoretical ways to cope in the moment, such as trying to understand that this other person might be taking some emotional challenge they're facing in another facet of their life out on them. That certainly isn't ok, but reminding yourself of this fact provides an opportunity for empathy and understanding. When being teased or ridiculed, having the awareness to understand that it's often rooted in jealousy and insecurity is challenging, but that awareness must be taught, the sooner the better.

Recognizing that things are often said out of ignorance is crucial too, especially growing up as a person of color. There was a moment at a play place when a young child asked then four-year-old Sarang if his relatives had accents, and said they hated accents because this is America and we speak English properly here. Irony aside, we were proud of the fact that he didn't react negatively in the moment. In fact, he told the kid that yes, in fact his relatives do have accents, and that's wonderful because they come from a different place that's just as lovely in different ways, and the other kid simply said "Oh, ok," and they continued playing. Maybe that kid learned something in that moment, maybe not, but that's beside the point. What matters is that Sarang, even at four, had the awareness to acknowledge that we live in a place where lots of people think and are taught differently, and oftentimes little kids' beliefs stem from the ignorance of their parents and other adults around them. Being able to run with that understanding, even in a moment when an angry reaction was entirely justified, shows a level of awareness we can all aspire toward.

It's one thing for a parent or teacher to provide comfort to a child, and another thing entirely to receive it from a friend. Being the one to give that comfort is an extra special kind of superpower, one that can be taught through awareness. Reading a room is tricky. Being on the lookout for feelings like sadness, worry, anger, etc. based on telling facial cues and reactions requires a level of awareness we adults often struggle to reach. Kids do it much more intuitively, and we should empower them by helping them be intentional about understanding these subtle signs.

There are so many stories we could highlight here. In week one of a new season of chorus, Sarang saw a new choirmate struggling to find their voice. He took the time to stop singing himself, walk over, and have a conversation with them, provide encouragement, acknowledge that he felt similarly his first time around, and emphasize that it'll get better. That evening, that child's mother came and told us what an impact this simple action made, and how excited her child was for future rehearsals. That's awareness. It's not only being aware of how the person across the room was feeling, but having the confidence and ability to realize that you, having experienced something similar not too long ago, might be able to share some comforting thoughts to support them, and that your support might propel your new friend to unexpected heights.

Another story happened at a chess tournament, when Sarang was in the final round, with a shot at anywhere between second and sixth place depending on how his last game went. His opponent was a year younger than him. In the waiting area before the round, Sarang overheard the child's father giving an impassioned speech about not hanging pieces and shooting your shot and whatnot. Sarang could see the child was a little off. When the pairings came out and Sarang saw they were playing one another, he took the kid under his wing. Rather than take advantage of their distracted state, he simply said if you just do your best and I do mine, we'll have a great game, and hopefully we both learn something, finish top five, and get some nice trophies.

At that moment, he made a friend. Ultimately his opponent made a mistake and Sarang ended up taking second. More important than the outcome, however, was the fact that Sarang walked with his opponent back to the room afterwards, sat down with them in front of their dad, and asked if they could go over the game together. They talked about things they could've done differently, shared stories about similar games they'd played, grew their new friendship, and in so doing perhaps helped show that parent that it's not so much about the result, but the learning and camaraderie and friendship. Again, I was struck by Sarang's situational awareness to recognize that his opponent was not feeling their best, and rather than take advantage of them, help empower them, even if it was ultimately at his own expense, and even help support them after the fact to change the perspective of their parent.

At some point between three and five, many organizations transition kids from the adult/child joint model to the child being solo. This transition can be very tough for some kids. It doesn't matter if the medium is dance, music, soccer, swimming, or any other activity. Separation anxiety is real, and the shift to independence and putting trust in a teacher rather than parent takes time. Not going to lie, it was tough for Sarang, but thanks to some friends who encouraged him, he ended up being just fine. More recently, we've had the pleasure of hearing numerous stories about how Vivaan had the awareness to ease this transition for his peers. He's in a place of relative comfort having already gone through it himself, not to mention also witnessing big brother do it first.

It's so sweet to witness Vivaan at work. The new kids come in, some clinging onto Mom's leg, others refusing to leave Grandpa's side. Vivaan knows, intuitively and by observation, to give them space, but also provide comfort and friendship when the time is right. As adults, we can go up to kids, introduce ourselves, ask their names, and be friendly. It's just not the same as when it comes from a kid, especially one the same age. It's so sweet to witness. He'll walk over, introduce himself, and ask their name. Then they'll exchange info on how old they are and when their birthday is, and he'll offer some thought as to why he loves whatever it is— chorus, swimming, chess, whatever—and how he's sure they'll love it to if they just give it a try. In addition to putting others at ease, it's a lovely way to make new friends, and it only takes a little awareness.

What's the Cost?

We'd all like our children to be able to navigate emotions thoughtfully. That said, we all have our own baggage and pet peeves, and they come out from time to time. Guess what? Our kids emulate us. So are their struggles to emotionally regulate partially our faults? Oh yeah. As for empathy, they see that, or the lack thereof, in us too. So yes, the cost in some ways is better managing our own human imperfections. Also, if you're the type to embarrass, reining that in is a major cost. If you exhibit ill feelings toward your child because of someone else's perception of them, that's 100% on you. It's not ok. They'll go further into their shell and struggle with emotional regulation even more. We need to be their strongest advocates, not their opposition. Broadly speaking, we need to keep working on ourselves, as they see and hear everything, so when they see us working on ourselves, they'll work on themselves too. It's really hard to do, but it needs to be done. Baby steps.

Self-awareness and awareness of those around you are important life skills that can be taught. The benefits of intentionally teaching kids both at a young age are far-reaching. Kids who are self-aware are able to navigate emotions more thoughtfully. Recognizing your own challenges and what bothers you can be a good first step in figuring out how to get over something, even if it's not your fault. Games are a great way to help kids articulate and manage their emotions in a low-stakes environment. Kids who are aware of those around them can choose to be empathetic, help a peer in a time of struggle, and make a friend in the process. Helping kids understand that they rarely know someone else's whole story, and oftentimes the actions of others are rooted in circumstances entirely unrelated to them, allows them to positively manage their reactions.

Vivaan's Reflection

Sometimes in swim class, people need help getting into the pool because they're feeling scared. I go over and help by saying "It's not that deep here, and I can hold your hand or maybe you can hold the teacher's hand." When they are scared to put their head under water, I say "Maybe start with your nose or ear then try your whole head and it's fun going under water." At chorus, sometimes kids won't leave their adult friends even though the adults are trying. I am always friendly and encourage my friends to join the fun.

Sarang's Reflection

My ears were very sensitive and I didn't like that people were making noise in an environment that was supposed to be silent. I used to get very upset because I would get distracted and focus is important during chess games. Sometimes I would ask arbiters to help and they tried but sometimes it didn't work and my opponents kept making noise when the arbiter walked away. Since then, I've really worked on tuning out the noise around me and focusing on my game even when those around me are making noise. I learned to take deep breaths, close my eyes briefly, calm my mind, and focus on what I can control. As for friends who are struggling with adjusting to new situations like singing in a group, I usually just say "you got this" and offer support. When I started new activities, I'd often feel nervous and it sometimes helps them to hear that from someone like me, who is now confident and comfortable in these environments.

Chapter Six
Resilience

Dad, I Can't Breathe. Am I Going to Die?

B efore delving into this important chapter on resilience, reflecting on one of the scariest experiences of our lives, we want to highlight that it is told from different perspectives deliberately as we were in different places at different times.

Siva's Reflection

It was an evening like any other. I was teaching downstairs. Aarti was with the boys upstairs. As I was finishing up with my last student for the night, I got a text from Aarti. "Sarang says he can't breathe." I rushed upstairs, and fortunately Aarti had the wherewithal to test him with the portable pulse oximeter we had in our medicine cupboard. His oxygen was low. Dangerously low. While my mind was racing a mile a minute, thinking of asthma, the horrific wildfire smog outside, hypoxia, brain damage, and yes, death, Aarti was already packing a bag to rush him to the E.R. Nothing like this had happened to him before. He was a mild asthmatic who took occasional albuterol at most. We gave him his puffer and he still couldn't muster the energy to get out of bed and walk down the stairs to the car. As I carried him to the car and was buckling him in, through his gasps, he said: "Dad I can't breathe. Am I going to die?"

At that moment, time stopped. My brain immediately went to a place of complete clarity. This was not the moment to be an educator. This was not the moment to talk about what might be and what might not. This was not a question from a kid seeking a rational conversation. We'd discussed death before. He knew all about it, and we'd even discussed what different faiths and traditions believe happened after. That was all irrelevant in this moment. This was a kid, a brilliant kid, who was fully aware that his ox levels were dangerously low, knew he felt a way he'd never felt before, and knew that if he did in fact stop breathing, he could die. He also knew this was a moment he had to fight, and he needed support from his dad. So what did I say? "Just breathe baby. Everything's going to be ok. Don't think or worry about anything. Just breathe. Mom's going to take you to the hospital, but I need you to fight. I need you to breathe. I believe in you, and I know you can do this. I'll be home with V right now but I'm always with you and I'll see you soon." In that instant our eyes met and he nodded, giving me this look of "Dad, I got this," and while I had absolutely no idea if everything was going to be ok, I knew that the conversation we just had was exactly what needed to happen in that moment.

When I returned upstairs, Vivaan was clearly shaken. "Daddy, is Sarang going to be ok? Is he going to die? I NEED my brother. What about Mommy? Is she going to tuck me in tonight?" We hugged. We snuggled. We talked. He processed. He concluded that his brother was the strongest kid he knew, a fighter, who could overcome any obstacle in his path. He concluded that he also had to be strong, resilient, and fight to support his brother from home. Though just four years old, he understood that Mommy time and brother time might be a lot less for a while. Daddy might have to tuck him in and help him sleep the next several nights, and that's ok. As I tucked him into bed and gave him a kiss, I think he could see the hand with my phone in it shaking while awaiting updates, along with the fear in my eyes, and he said: "Daddy, it's going to be ok."

Aarti's Reflection

It was a typical Thursday evening and my brother and his wife were over to hang out and have dinner with me and the boys. Usually, Sarang does not waste a minute after dinner before dragging his uncle down to play video games. However, this evening, he quietly ate his dinner and crawled into his bed. Noticing his absence, I went to his room to check in on him and he said, "Mom, I'm so tired. I'm having a hard time breathing. I just want to sleep." This had never happened before. In fact, Sarang normally has a really hard time calming down and sticking to his bedtime routine – so all the warning bells went off in my head. That's when I texted Siva to alert him that something was wrong.

I left Siva with Sarang for a few minutes, left Vivaan with my brother and his wife, and quickly packed an overnight bag for the hospital. Siva helped load Sarang into the car, and then we were on our way to the hospital. I turned up the classical music station and Sarang and I listened to Dvorak's symphony on the way to the ER. I used the twenty-minute ride to prep him for what he could expect at the ER, and reassured him that I loved him and that I'd be with him the whole time he was at the hospital. I also told him over and over again that the people working in the hospital would know exactly how to help him and that I was very proud of how calm he was being at that moment. He did not ask whether he was going to die again – he just nodded his head, and took labored breaths in the back seat.

When we got into the ER, it was a new adventure for Sarang. Every wheelchair ride became a cool Mario Kart race in his head. He kept track of every single person who came to work with him, from the triage nurses to the residents, fellows, and attendings. He was very curious about how they were helping him breathe better, and what each machine around him did. He was able to completely shift his mindset from the one of panic that he had experienced merely 30 minutes ago to one of great curiosity. He was also tickled pink that we stayed awake in the ER until 5:00 a.m. – the latest his bedtime ever had been! Unfortunately, the treatments administered in the ER weren't sufficient, and he had to spend several days in the hospital to make a full recovery.

Siva's Reflection

In the days and weeks that followed, it was tough. Really tough. Sarang made it to the hospital in time and sure enough, he had suffered a serious asthma attack, and would need to be hospitalized for several days. While we "did all the right things," we were still beating ourselves up about what we could've done better. We also vowed to be even more prepared next time, should such a serious thing happen again. We switched off at the hospital periodically, though Aarti did the bulk of the heavy lifting there, our family nearby stepped up to help at home as needed, as we were managing these challenges. Curiously, and most amazingly, the person who was managing best mentally, though his body was still fighting to breathe, was Sarang.

When I walked into that hospital ward the following morning and saw Sarang safely asleep, connected to all sorts of machines that were helping him breathe, I let out a huge sigh of relief. When he woke, I saw his smile. He couldn't talk much, as he'd go into a coughing fit, but he gave me a thumbs up and did manage to say "I love it here." Gradually his coughing went down, his oxygen levels up, and every time a member of the hospital staff came in, they told me about their interactions with Sarang. "You have quite a kid there." "He's so aware of everything we're doing and so curious about what we do." "He would make a great doctor." "He would make a great nurse." "We'll never forget him." A few days after the initial scare and still in the hospital, though thankfully out of the ER, Sarang and I had an amazing conversation. He told me about every machine in his hospital room and what it does. He told me about everyone who came in, their names, what they do, and why they do it. He told me he absolutely adored Seattle Children's and wondered when he'd be going back. He also loved the unlimited TV, Nintendo Switch, and food on demand.

After a while he returned home, and for the next three weeks we stayed put, didn't do any activities, didn't meet anyone, and just focused on Sarang regaining his health. Vivaan was so excited to have his brother home, but also immediately understood that he shouldn't play rough at this time. While Sarang was eager to resume all his activities with his friends, he also knew how he felt. He was aware of his challenges in the moment, and knew that rest was critical to overcome them. Sure enough, after about a month, life resumed as normal, and all was well.

The major cost here is the fact that often resilience is built through adverse experiences. No parent wants to expose their kids to adversity. That said, the world will do that to them: every kid will face challenges. When they do, how we approach them as parents makes a major difference to our kids. If we view every setback as an opportunity, and every challenge as an adventure, however scary or dangerous it might be, they'll likely do the same. They watch us. Moreover, allowing them to fail, and learn to overcome failure in a safe, controlled environment at home will also help tremendously when they're facing the real life stuff that's out of their control. You can do this. It's hard. But you can do this.

Siva's Reflection

Firstly, parenting instinct is real, and trusting it is important. Kids are incredibly self-aware, and trusting them is crucial. Kids can step up to whatever challenge they're facing, however hard it may be. Resilience is a key life skill to be taught, and that teaching starts at home. It's ok to be scared. It's ok to be worried. It's even better to acknowledge that those are the emotions you're feeling, and to know when it's time to fight. I was especially impressed at Sarang's calm, and willingness to just breathe. I don't know if I would have had the wherewithal to do that at age eight. How did he build this resilience? How did he know it was time to be a Gryffindor, as he would say? I think it really starts with letting children take chances, early and often, make mistakes and learn from them, and get messy and learn to clean up, as Ms. Frizzle used to say on the Magic School Bus. Doing that in a relatively controlled, safe environment throughout their childhood empowers them to do the same when the real challenges hit.

The love of learning is everything for a child. It is our job as parents to facilitate it, nurture it, encourage it, and do everything in our power to not diminish it. At no point during this ordeal did Sarang believe it was an ordeal. In fact, he felt it was a new adventure, a new experience, a new challenge. Mentally, he was loving learning about hospitals, the people who worked there, the machines, and more, while physically his body was fighting. When he finally came off the oxygen and had his hands free to play Switch, he told me he was going to get the world record on his favorite Mario Kart track, Mushroom Gorge. I said go for it. He didn't quite get the world record, but he did get a global top twenty time, oxygen cannulas, low energy, cough, and all.

Aarti's Reflection

For me, this story is an important reminder that children will mirror your behavior, especially when in crisis mode. While I was internally panicked throughout this experience, I tried my very best to appear calm, spoke reassuring words, and clearly communicated what I knew and what I didn't know in the face of uncertainty. I also checked in often with Sarang during his stay, to see if he had any questions about his treatment plan. Most hospital rooms have a place to record patient questions, and we talked a lot during our stay about what we wanted to ask the hospital staff the next time they visited our room. The whole time, I was also extremely aware of what Vivaan needed from me. I insisted that Siva switch with me for at least a few hours during the day so that I could come home, shower, and spend some time playing with Vivaan and giving him an update on Sarang. Those few hours of respite allowed me to recharge and be strong for Sarang. While I wasn't there to tuck Vivaan in many nights in a row, I continued a lot of our other little rituals whenever I was home. Lastly, all of this would have been nearly impossible to navigate without the support of our family and friends. We had an outpouring of support from our community, and were extremely thankful for that.

Vivaan's Reflection

I was so proud of Sarang for fighting. I couldn't go to the hospital because I wasn't sick and Covid was happening, but every night Dad and I had a video call with Mommy and Sarang. Even though he couldn't talk a lot and was sick, it felt so good to see my Ba (brother) and know he would be ok. Mommy would come home and play with me a few hours every day and Daddy and I had fun too. After he got home, it was a little different since he couldn't run around or play outside but we still had a lot of fun playing Switch, chatting, doing puzzles, eating together, and playing games.

That experience was my most Gryffindor moment ever! I'm mostly a Ravenclaw but after that, I might be a Ravendor! In the car ride to the hospital I was pretty scared but then I thought "I can do this" and I'm going to treat this like the final Bowser fight in Mario and fight hard. I got a wheelchair ride (my Mario Kart!) in and on the way to the ER I saw an advertisement of my grandma holding a baby. That was so cool! The hospital was so fun! They had my usual oatmeal for breakfast, sandwiches, cookies, and lots of good food. Lots of new friends, about 50, came into my room during my time there, and I loved chatting with them and hearing stories about their lives and what they do. The machines around me were so cool! There was a monitor connected to me showing my pulse, O_2 levels, and blood pressure. It would beep whenever my O_2 levels dropped below 90%. That happened a lot in the first few days. I had to take puffers all the time, had different kinds of oxygen masks, and Mom was so great reading me books and helping me get snacks and go to sleep. Oh yeah, I had my best time trial ever at the hospital. It was an absolutely crazy moment and probably the hospital world record! I used my favorite character at the time, Yoshi (now it's Dry Bones), in the Biddybuggy with roller tires and a cloud glider, hit all the shortcuts on Mushroom Gorge, and got a global top twenty time! Overall it was a really fun experience.

Chapter Seven
Privilege

Can I Donate My Chess Prize Money?

P rivilege can be a challenging concept to navigate, especially as a young learner who's gradually becoming more self-aware and aiming to take ownership of their actions. Before the Covid-19 pandemic began, Sarang had just started playing chess tournaments. He was improving and had received a few medals and trophies that he displayed in his room. With in-person activities no longer an option, chess tournaments transitioned online, and with that, physical medals and trophies turned into gift cards and money, which could be easily emailed. Over the course of the pandemic, Sarang received around $500 in prize money. With his first monetary prize, he decided to buy a gift for his brother and a chess book for himself, so he could continue to improve. As the money continued to come in, he reflected his desire to continue giving gifts, as well as an investment in his own learning, when he asked us: "Can I donate my chess prize money?"

Philanthropy has always been at the forefront of our minds, as reasonably privileged, conscious citizens and parents who have ample means for ourselves and our children. At least once a year, we'd sit down as a family and discuss causes and groups doing great work and give what we could to them. When Sarang asked us this question, we were ecstatic. Besides the "of course" response, what followed was a lovely discussion about what he believes in, who he wants to help, and the impact of giving—however small the amount might be—all culminating in the realization that ultimately it was on him to think about what causes he cared about most deeply, and how to help them. As he researched causes, it became more and more apparent to him that the world was anything but a fair place, and that those of us dealt a better hand should do something about that. I think it really hit home when he saw kids lacking the funds to go to school, learn to read, get toys or clean clothes, and even have clean water, let alone travel, explore museums, and participate in lots of activities as he did. Moreover, witnessing their sheer joy at these simplest of things, things we often take for granted, was powerful.

Through his research, he discovered several organizations helping young people. He found an organization helping feed hungry families in India and provide them with clean clothing. He found an organization providing books and academic support to kids whose parents might not have the means to do so. He found an organization that provided care and support to foster children. He found an organization that provided pediatric medical care to those uninsured and fighting homelessness. He found organizations that would accept donations of gently used toys, which allowed him to give some of his possessions, in addition to money. He gave, and did so generously, learning as he did.

I remember him asking me one day if he was doing enough, giving enough, and helping enough, and expressing disappointment that there was no way he could give in the amounts we did, or the way millionaires or billionaires could, nor help in the same way. In that moment, we had a heart to heart, and I made it very clear to him that he's doing far more than I ever did at his age, that the fact that he was giving well over than half of what he earned was something Mom and Dad could only aspire toward, and that as he grew, he'd make more so he could give more. He was inspiring us. We also discussed how serving others is a mindset and way of living. It's not just about money. Shortly thereafter, whenever anyone even came over to help us at home, a delivery person, a housecleaner, an electrician, a gardener, or a contractor, he'd happily go chat and ask if they had kids and if they'd like any of his toys or books. As the joy in giving grew, he realized too that not only money and physical gifts were needed, but mental gifts, like sharing knowledge, exchanging smiles, listening to stories, telling stories, teaching, and more.

When those epiphanous moments happened, true empathy developed, and it was magical. He became a better brother. He became a better friend. He became a better student. He became a better person. When he saw the new kid at chorus struggling to fit in, he went over to comfort them, and not only made a new friend, but also helped instill some confidence in them that they otherwise may not have seen, to help them overcome their initial challenges. At chess tournaments, as they gradually returned to being in person, he helped players find their boards, offered new parents guidance on where to wait between rounds, helped new players understand notation and how to use the clocks, and helped his peers and new friends analyze their games as best as he could, to help them improve. When a crisis struck, whether with family or friends or even acquaintances we were familiar with, he'd be the first to say "How can we help?" and do what he could. Selfish desires decreased. When he wanted the fancy new toy, he did a doubletake and thought maybe we could do something better with this.

Now you may be thinking, surely this kid has it all. Yes. He does. He'll get plenty of gifts and toys, learn from so many, including us, and have opportunities many can only dream of. That said, to me it matters most that he recognizes that, owns that, and uses his privilege, platform, and ultimately power for service and good. Fascinatingly, when this process began for Sarang, it was already firmly ingrained in baby, then toddler, Vivaan's mind.

Vivaan is singularly the most empathetic person in our family. He constantly gives, and tries to help as best as he can. When another kiddo in his activities is having a meltdown, he'll try to be a shoulder to cry on, or the one to share a smile or comforting hug. He exudes this empathy to those around them, including Sarang, and helps us all be more giving and kind. Now, some may attribute this to childish ignorance, and while he may not yet fully understand money or fiscal responsibility the way the rest of us do, and may overdo it from time to time from the heady adult perspective, I think the world might be a little better off if more people acted with their heart first rather than head. We can all learn a lot from the kindness and selfless love of young children.

I was particularly touched one day when Vivaan was at the local chess club. He was the youngest player in the tournament of the day, by a good margin, and between rounds he was acutely aware of the siblings of other kids playing, who were largely ignored and often bored, but nonetheless clearly eager to learn what their sibs were doing. I watched as he went from person to person, offering to share his knowledge of chess: how the pieces move, how much they're worth, and how fun it can be. It was so cool seeing their eyes light up, and even more wonderful to see the joy in his own eyes at helping his new friends out. He taught toddlers, kids, teens, and adults alike. This wasn't about age. It was about a kid who recognized the emotions and needs of those around him, perhaps seeing something of himself not that long ago in them, and doing what he could to help. It got to the point where wherever we'd go, we'd have a chessboard and pieces with us, so that if the boys saw someone looking bored, they could pull out a board and offer up a game or a lesson! It happened at swim practice. It happened at choir practice. It happened at band practice. It happened at tennis practice. It happened everywhere! Sarang and Vivaan became known as the chess boys wherever they went, and spread their love of the game with so many who might not have even considered trying it.

What's the Cost?

Honestly, we don't think there is one, but navigating privilege and philanthropy is tricky. Perhaps they become too giving and may struggle with fiscal responsibility? You can help them with that and find the right balance. As for recognizing and acknowledging privilege, yes it's tricky, and with it may come some guilt. Helping kids realize that being privileged is no reason to feel guilty, but rather an opportunity to serve, helps with that element. Using metaphors with cards or games can help too. Make it less personal if needed. Maybe you're dealt two Kings in a game of Blackjack. Maybe someone else is dealt a two and a six. Think those are equal? Also, providing some language and context around privilege will help tremendously in preventing entitlement, a pandemic in its own right.

Siva's Reflection

We can't help but feel thankful not only for all the gifts we have as a family, but also the opportunities we have to serve and give back. It's wonderful to see the kids developing this sense of service, as well as a deeper understanding that not everyone is dealt an equal hand, and that those of us holding pocket aces can simultaneously be thankful for it, learn from it, and empower those who weren't so lucky. It was also lovely to see the gradual progression from selfishness to selflessness, and how quickly it happened for Vivaan. As a lifelong educator, it was particularly touching to see the boys' desire to teach, and help those around them join them on their journeys of being lifelong lovers of learning, whether through the medium of music, chess, or otherwise. I think through giving tangible and intangible things, they also developed a much keener sense of the world around them, their place in it, and a better sense of themselves.

Aarti's Reflection

I remember volunteering from a very young age. While most of my friends had summer jobs all through high school, I spent most of my summers volunteering at the American Red Cross and other organizations. Even when I was in college, I found time amid my taxing schoolwork and my three jobs to volunteer in the arts community. Today, we involve the kids every time we make a giving decision, and model how they can use their privilege for good by volunteering in their chess and music communities. Seattle has a significant population experiencing homelessness, and when the kids ask questions about how people end up in these situations, we have honest conversations with them and ideate with them on how we can be more responsible in our communities. I also spend a lot of time reading stories to them about helpful characters – story tales and folklore are filled with examples of kindness and goodwill. If you're not much of a storyteller, leverage kids' podcasts, TV shows, or school events so that they have lots of different examples in their lives of how to be a positive part of a community.

Vivaan's Reflection

Working hard and helping people are very important. I can tell from someone's eyes if they are feeling sad or bored and when they are, I try to do something they will like to help them feel better. One time at chess club, I saw a Mom and her two- or three-year-old daughter sitting in a corner while my Dad and brother were still playing their games. I went over and asked if they wanted to learn chess and they said yes! I told them the pieces, how they move, and some strategy and soon they were playing! It felt good to be able to make new friends and teach them something new.

I am very lucky. I live in a comfortable house, have a loving family, do lots of activities, have good food, clean clothes, and rarely have to struggle. As I started receiving prize money, I tried to think more about other people and how I could help. I really wanted to help those who are experiencing homelessness, kids who need food and education, and those who are sick. I gave most of the money I won to those who need it more and began helping in other ways too. I wrote letters to veterans experiencing homelessness, I collected food for food drives, I got books and clothes for donation drives, and more. I'm doing my best to do what I can now but definitely want to do more as I grow up. Also if anyone wants to learn some chess or music, my brother and I would love to teach you!

<u>Chapter Eight</u>
Confidence

Can I Make My Own Birthday Cake?

O ver the years, we've had the privilege of working with and befriending numerous movers and shakers, who are changing the world in a variety of ways. When we chat with them about what it takes to thrive in this world, a consistent message is the importance of confidence. So how do we instill confidence in our kids? How do we give them the confidence to take ownership of their actions?

As a four-year-old, Vivaan developed a strong affinity for cooking, and in particular baking. He helped both of us in the kitchen several times every week and loved experimenting with new and avant-garde ideas, which, as foodies, we were excited to try. A few weeks before his fifth birthday he asked us, "Can I bake my own birthday cake?" We were delighted to oblige, knowing that, thanks to the work he had put in, he now had the self-confidence to give this a try. We simply inquired how we could help. So over the next week he came up with a gameplan. He researched ingredients and different types of cakes before eventually concluding that he wanted to prepare a Pink Lady apple cinnamon vanilla cake. He'd made cakes before. He'd made doughnuts and cookies and all sorts of other pastries too. But this one was extra special to him, as he wanted to make it on his birthday, for his family, and take ownership of the whole process, start to finish.

The day before his birthday, he realized we only had Opal apples. While they were delicious, they simply wouldn't provide the flavor he envisioned, so we set out to get a couple of Pink Ladies. We did have real vanilla, which as you may recall was a revelation, and became a rather critical ingredient in his cooking after the Belize trip when he first experienced it. We also had fresh cinnamon. As for our help, he wanted us to be his assistants. We peeled and grated the Pink Ladies, and stuck the cake in the oven after he'd made sure all the quantities were perfect and done all the mixing. After an hour in the oven, we took it out and let it cool, that sweet apple cinnamon-y aroma wafting throughout our humble home. When the time came to cut the first slice, it was perfect. The consistency was perfect. The sugar was perfect.

Most importantly, the love and planning and confidence it took for the newly minted five-year-old to do this, on his birthday no less, was beyond perfect.

Switching kiddos and mediums that give them confidence, by age six, Sarang was utterly infatuated with data. He poured over it, analyzed it, and became quite quantitatively literate. Perhaps because he saw us involved with the 2016 election, he became interested in the 2020 election. It was about a year and a half before the election, and candidates were beginning to think about running. The primaries were on the horizon, so there was lots of data coming out from polls. One day, he asked us "Why can't I vote?" We responded that the law states you must be 18 years old to vote, and when further prodded why, we couldn't give a good answer. The reality was that this kid was far more politically literate at age six than many adults. He followed up his initial question by asking what he could do. We turned it back on him, as we do, and he decided to launch a political podcast. His goal was to inform listeners and viewers about what the data said, how reliable it was, and what to expect moving forward. And he did exactly that, nearly weekly, over the next year-and-a-half, through Election Day.

The amount of learning that happened during his political podcaster phase was remarkable, as was watching him grow in confidence and gradually come out of his shell. Every week he'd do his research, create a PowerPoint, and write a script. He'd then record the script, blend the visual slides with the relevant audio, render it, and post it. Again, he was six when this started. His audience quickly grew until several hundred folks, mostly family and friends, would watch what he had to say. When we met them, he'd have deep, thoughtful conversations about politics, trying his best to stay rational and base his ideas on data, rather than emotion, contrary to how adults often converse about politics. He became a better planner, speaker, writer, and communicator. More than anything, by doing this work, a little bit every day, he became a much more confident individual, who realized there is a place for his voice even though so many might discount him due to his age.

Fast forward to 2023. The nine- and five-year-old boys are about to play in a chess tournament to support a local nonprofit. By now you know chess is a passion for both and they are consistently working at studying the game, as well as having a blast playing it. In the days leading up to the tournament, they saw that they were both among the stronger players in their respective fields, and set themselves the goals of playing their best, having fun, making friends, and not getting phased when they fail. Oh, and going 5/5 and winning the tournament. The usual stretch goal thing. They did the prep work, and they were ready.

Round one they both won. Round two they both won. Leading up to round three, they knew they'd be facing stiffer competition. They both won again. At 3/3, they were both up to board one, the top board of their respective sections. They were confident. They knew they were playing very strong competition, but they also knew they were strong. Perhaps the glint of the trophies that had been laid out at the front of the gymnasium inspired a little too much confidence, but both lost.

3/4 apiece. As you've been reading this chapter, the question of if there's a thing as too much confidence may have come up. No doubt. Overconfidence, arrogance, and even cockiness are real. Hopefully our boys don't possess those attributes, and if they do, we trust they will have ample opportunities, like this one, to be sufficiently humbled. Can you guess how they felt after their losses? Yeah. Not great. That said, they didn't melt down. They didn't pout. They congratulated their opponents, dusted themselves off, and got their blood flowing to ready themselves for the final round. While the top prizes were out of reach, they knew that with a strong performance, they'd still be able to leave with their heads held high, knowing they'd given their all. Oh, and they might still be in line for some hardware, even if not the biggest.

They both won their final games, Vivaan earning his first-ever 4/5 in a tournament, and Sarang earning the same, a score he'd achieved many times. They congratulated each another and as the remaining games finished, they also congratulated their friends and awaited the awards ceremony. Turns out they both tied for second in their respective sections, with Vivaan earning the second place trophy in his section and Sarang earning the third place trophy in his. Confidence came in clutch. So did resilience. So did their self-awareness. It was particularly lovely to see them going around congratulating their buddies and taking pictures with them.

One final story, highlighting the power of confidence, centers around a recent tennis experience. Siva loved tennis growing up, and through college it was a major part of his life. Sarang began lessons at age seven, and came to love it as he learned from Siva's old coach, a truly transcendent, generational teacher who worked hard to inspire confidence in all they worked with.

During the pandemic, we bought a portable net and began playing wherever we could find a large patch of concrete or asphalt. Vivaan began to express interest. By four, he was excitedly holding a racket and trying to volley, or at the very least be an amazing ball kid for his brother and dad. At the tennis club, during Sarang's lesson, Vivaan would insist on going outside and playing catch or keepy uppy, or practicing his ready position, forehand motion, and backhand motion with Dad.

One day, Vivaan went up to the front desk and asked when he could start taking classes. They said he needed to be five, because 75-minute classes are long, tiring, and require lots of patience. He mentioned he was already playing chess tournaments, so he felt ready. His next question was how long the waitlist to get in was. They said six to eight months. At the time, he was nearly four and a half, and perfectly capable of basic arithmetic. Alright then, let's put my name on the waitlist now, so I can start as soon as I turn five! Surprised but appreciative of his enthusiasm, confidence, and awareness, they said ok.

Word spread to the coaches, and whenever they saw him practicing outside, they offered encouragement, and mentioned how excited they were to work with him once he turned five. He improved. He began hitting some groundstrokes. He was getting more control. His fifth birthday came, and he eagerly went to every one of Sarang's practices to ask if he could begin lessons himself. They said they still needed a spot to open, but were hopeful he would have one in the next few months. Then, one morning a few weeks after he turned five, an email came. A spot just opened for Vivaan! Thanks so much for your patience. Would he like it? Of course he would! The kid was over the moon!

That evening, he joined his brother at the club, this time as a student. After getting his temperature checked, per protocol, Sarang took him down to the court, where Vivaan happily reintroduced himself to the coaches and mentioned that it was his first time, and he was so excited to learn. Siva's coach, equally enthusiastic, proudly proclaimed that this kid was another legacy, just turned five, and that he used to coach his Dad, and was currently coaching his brother! It was a lovely evening. Was Vivaan exhausted after his first 75-minute practice? No doubt. That said, he was ready for the challenge. He had a blast. He learned a lot. As for his confidence? There was a moment during class where he hit three consecutive beautiful backhands! His coach said: "Dude, your backhand is amazing!" He was positively beaming, and during the car ride home asked when he could practice some more to get ready for the next class.

Honestly, it's hard to find one here. Perhaps it's the adult ego, and the belief that we're always, or even usually, right when it comes to what's best for our kids. We need to acknowledge that our little ones are their own people with interests and passions that may deviate from our own, and empowering that deviation is critical to building their confidence. We need to teach them self-advocacy skills by encouraging them to take the lead. Admittedly, ceding control can be challenging. Perhaps you have the fear that they might become arrogant jerks. While this fear might be rooted in some of our own bad experiences, the reality is that when a child has firmly embraced a growth mindset, the humility is embedded. The confidence will simply help their self-image, work ethic, and yes, performance.

Aarti and Siva's Reflections

If kids are given the space to run with what they're into, experiment, practice, and improve, their confidence will grow, and with that confidence they can take ownership of their learning and do some rather remarkable things. Confidence also requires patience, and ideally an aversion to incessant comparison, something that plagues far too many people. So will Vivaan become a chef and Sarang a politician? Probably not. Will they become professional chess players? Unlikely. That said, in those moments, they had put in the work and built up their confidence to do some rather awesome things at very young ages, despite societal messaging of you're too young for this or that. As parents, educators, friends, or other family members, our job is to empower the kids in our lives to grow their confidence. Without confidence, self-doubt may creep in, and that insidiousness may only worsen over time, as they approach puberty and beyond. As a high school educator for well over a decade, Siva witnessed this happen far too often. The funny thing is, the source of the confidence doesn't matter—it could be x, y, or z. Confident kids, whatever their source, believe in themselves, and that prompts a stronger work ethic, and better performance.

Are some kids overconfident? Absolutely. But the world has a way of quickly humbling said overconfidence. So what concrete things can we do to help empower their confidence while not letting it reach the point of arrogance or cockiness? Give kids the space to experiment with and practice their passions, even if they're not in line with what you believe will serve them well in their adult lives in the distant future. If their passions change, which they will, roll with it. Let them find their respective lanes. Maybe music will help your kids find their voice. Maybe cooking. Maybe chess. Maybe basketball. Maybe even video games. It really doesn't matter. If a child finds a lane that helps them grow in their self-love, self-respect, and self-confidence, encourage them in it, as their confidence in that one lane will eventually spread to nearly all areas of their lives. Once it does, they'll be more willing to try new things, take thoughtful risks, and practice to get better, knowing that they've done it before in whatever lanes they chose in the past. As for averting going overboard and teetering on the edge of cockiness, so long as they can see there's still room for growth and that the race is theirs alone, they will keep progressing and find the necessary humility to balance their confidence, knowing there's still so far to go.

Vivaan's Reflection

Cooking is pretty easy for me and I love it. I like it because there are simple steps I can follow and make something super yummy with my family. As I've grown, I can do more and more in the kitchen by myself. I try to practice every day because that helps me get better. I felt great getting 4/5 for the first time and earning a 2nd place trophy in a Kindergarten 1st grade section even though I'm only pre-K age. Going into my games, I felt readier than ever. I had studied and prepared and my tactics were getting a lot better. I love tennis. I watched Sarang learning and now I get to learn too! I got a rally of twenty shots with my Dad and I love practicing! As I learn and practice and get better, I believe in myself more and more, and that's confidence!

Sarang's Reflection

Thanks to my political podcasting career, I am now confident in analyzing data, sharing knowledge both spoken and written, and more confident talking with adults about "adult" things. I did over thirty episodes over four seasons, and watching them back it was awesome to see how much I improved with more and more practice. I am a confident person. I believe in myself. It's because I work hard and can see the improvement that comes with it. I've seen so much growth in my video games, tennis, chess, singing, piano, drums, coding, basketball, puzzling, building, and even as a brother.

Chapter Nine
Goals

Can I Play Chess Tournaments Too?

S arang was having a chess lesson in the living room and solving some tactics puzzles. Finding himself in an interesting position, he wasn't too sure about what move to pick, and said so out loud. Vivaan, who was playing with Magnatiles nearby, thought it was a question for him, rushed to the board, and immediately found the right move!

Now let's backtrack a little bit. Chess has been a major part of our life for a while. We love the community, the challenge, and the facilitation of numerous mental habits that benefit learning and life in general: taking turns, patience, spatial reasoning, planning, number sense, sportsmanship, decision-making under uncertainty, and resilience. Sarang began learning chess when he was three. He saw Siva playing and expressed interest. He began playing tournaments when he was six. Soon after, Siva worked on a major grant project to use chess as a medium to bridge the kindergarten readiness gap. Naturally we beta tested it on toddler Vivaan. He picked it up very quickly. Fast forward a few weeks and we're at a chess tournament. Sarang is playing and Vivaan and Siva are waiting in the hallway, chatting and solving simple chess puzzles on a little board. These tournaments last all day (if not multiple days), and in the early afternoon Vivaan asked what we thought we wouldn't hear for a couple of years at least: "Can I play chess tournaments too?"

Of course, our minds were buzzing. Can we really put our three-year-old in chess tournaments? Is he patient enough? Can he cope with the emotional challenge of losing? Despite those concerns, he's coming to the events anyway, so why not let him play? We started playing more "tournament games" at home to see how he'd react, by modeling playing in silence, focusing, and even using a chess clock. He'd have Siva, Aarti, or Sarang "play like a Kindergartner or first grader." He'd win some. He'd lose some. He did not like losing, and would often melt down. Shortly thereafter, he asked if he could also take lessons with my brother from another, a chess Master and dear friend I used to coach with back in the day. This was the first sign to us that he was getting closer to being ready. He wanted to learn. He wanted to study. He wanted to get better.

At first, his sessions were just ten minutes, before Sarang's lesson each week. Quickly, they grew to a half hour. He was into it, absorbing information at an incredible rate. That said, emotionally, he wasn't ready. So, we reached an agreement. When he learned to lose, to Siva, to Aarti, to Sarang, to whomever, he could be a little sad, but he shouldn't melt down, and should instead view the loss as an opportunity to learn. When that happened, he could play tournaments.

Vivaan's goal was to be ready to compete in September 2022, so he could have two full years playing Kindergarten events. Remarkably, by March, just a couple months after this process began, he was ready. He viewed losses as learning opportunities, and though he much preferred winning and the prospect of shiny medals and trophies, he was learning a lot and improving quickly, and those were great feelings. He played a couple tournaments, and performed well enough to qualify for the State Championships! It was his first ever big tournament, against mostly kids two years older than him. While he lost most of his games, he won some, and finished in the top 20, earning a medal, with two more years in that K section still to go!

Fast forward to the fall of 2022. Both boys are playing in a National Open. Sarang is playing in the K-3 Open, a section he took second in last year. Vivaan is playing it for the first time, in the K-1 U800 section. As the day progresses, we are truly struck by the parallels between the boys, in spite of their being at wildly different levels of chess. Both love the game. Both use it as a medium to think deeply and learn. Both use it as a way to connect and make friends. Between every round they're running around and having fun with their buddies. Sure, there's some chess analysis going on, but by and large it's social. It's fun. It's joy. More than that, the results of the event aren't driving that joy. Playing is the joy. Spending time with friends is the joy. Making new friends is the joy. It's lovely. The tournament finishes up and both take 11th in their sections, each winning more than they lost. Could they have done better chess wise? Sure. That said, they played well, had fun, spent time with friends, made new ones, and learned a lot. They also both qualified for State in the spring of 2023, Vivaan still in K (though Pre-K age now) and Sarang in third grade.

A month later, the boys were invited to compete in a local school tournament. We're big fans of school-sponsored tournaments, as they're an opportunity to help fundraise for a club, and for lots of newer players to gain some valuable tournament experience. This particular event was wild. The previous five days it had snowed, in Bellevue, Washington, in the fall. Climate change. The parking lot was a bit of a slip 'n slide, as was the path to the playing hall, in spite of all the efforts to keep it clear. Despite the weather challenges, I'd never seen an event with more enthusiasm and genuine love for chess. Everyone was all smiles, whether in the playing hall, skittles room (where people wait after games), or even outside playing soccer in the snow! Deep, thoughtful conversations were everywhere, around chess, schooling, and life in general. Games were played, not only chess, but also Uno, cards, puzzles, Connect 4, and more. When the time came for each round to begin, players went to play, had a blast, then returned for even more fun. After all five rounds were complete, it was so cool to see all the players hanging out and reveling in the friendships they'd made over the course of the day. Were they excited about the trophies and medals to come? Sure. In the moment, those are nice tangible tokens of a job well done, but long-term they're really a memory capsule, transporting these young minds back to those moments of joy and friendship. Ultimately our boys did quite well, with Sarang taking second in the K-3 Open and Vivaan taking 7th in the K-1 U800, his first ever top-ten finish and non-participation-based trophy.

What's the Cost?

Like with many things, time, and perhaps disappointment if unrealistic goals and expectations are set. Starting something new in your likely already "overcommitted" lives is hard. It takes time. It takes resources. It also provides opportunity. Be calculated about it. Find things that are within your means that interest your child. Let them take the lead. Set goals, and keep them reasonable. If pie-in-the-sky goals are more your family's style, let your child have some, but also have them make some more concrete, achievable goals that you know they can do, and do fairly quickly to make it clear to them that they're progressing. Perception is everything. Comparing them to the best and brightest in the activity doesn't help anyone. Comparing them to themselves a week ago? Before their lesson to after their lesson? That can be useful, and help them understand that they're growing and making progress. The only one in the race is them.

While their chess journeys are just beginning, the friendships they've made, the lessons they've learned, and the habits of mind they've developed so far have been truly extraordinary. The clear takeaway is the importance of running with a child's curiosity. When a child is curious about something, run with that curiosity, and afford them what opportunities you can to help them explore it. Readiness is a tricky thing to self-assess. Being the support mechanism for your child to help them come up with a game plan for when they're ready to try something new is important. It might be a couple of leading questions, or a few concrete goals you can think of together that they must achieve to jump in. In this case, those goals were learning how to lose, not melting down in the process, and viewing every loss as a learning opportunity. Goal-setting is a challenge we all navigate, but an especially trying one for a child. Pie in the sky goals are fine, but helping them come up with concrete, achievable goals that are ideally not strictly results-focused can make a world of difference, not only in their development in the activity, but also in their self-confidence and ownership.

As for chess specifically, give it a try. It's a beautiful game that, for a child, may be the single most powerful source of learning how to confidently make rational decisions under uncertainty, a skill that's proved invaluable in our lives. It doesn't matter if you play or not. In fact, while Aarti knew the basics of the game from her childhood, she never spent much time playing until the boys came along and expressed interest. Go on to ChessKid, take some lessons online, watch some YouTube videos, learn the names of the pieces, learn about the board, learn how the pieces move, solve some simple puzzles, build your vocabulary and your knowledge. These baby steps will help your child enormously. If it feels like something they might pursue a bit more, take some lessons in person. Join a chess club. The community is incredibly collaborative, and while there are competitive elements as in any sport or game, the ultimate goal is shared love of the game and growth. Did you know after a game, typically the winner will offer to go over the game, and in analyzing together, grow collective understanding and make a friend? What other sport offers that? Give chess a try. You won't regret it.

Vivaan's Reflection

I learned how to play chess when I was two. I first learned the names of the chess pieces then the names of the squares on the chess board. Then I learned how the pieces move. I went to tournaments a lot with my brother and I had to wait outside. It was kind of boring waiting. When I turned three, I wanted to play tournaments too. Dad was surprised. When I lost at home, I got upset and knocked over the pieces. Now I don't do that. Now when I lose I shake hands, say good game, and try to learn from it. Now I'm playing in chess tournaments, having fun, making friends, and get trophies and medals! I am excited for more chess!

Sarang's Reflection

I started learning chess at three. I learned over the next three years with Uncle Josh and Dad. Through the pandemic, I played a lot of chess, made lots of friends, and even published articles reflecting on my chess experiences. We had a team of buddies called the Bhandar Bhais, which literally means monkey bros in Hindi, and we played Mini Team tournaments run by Dad and had a blast. Chess has also allowed me to build confidence, travel for tournaments, and have lots of fun. One of the best things about chess is teaching my bro. We do lots of fun puzzles and games and it's so cool that he's playing tournaments already! I'm super excited about all the chess fun to come.

Chapter Ten
Readiness

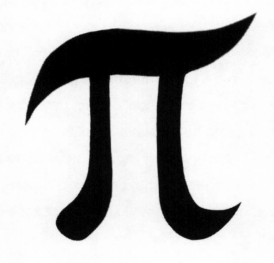

Can You Teach Me Calculus?

A ssessing readiness may be one of the most challenging aspects of parenting. There is an overabundance of information out there, including checklists full of information from doctors, friends, grandparents, other family members, and more, not to mention those pesky letters you get in the mail with "Does your n year old do this?" giving parents the opportunity to pat themselves on the back, freak out, cheer, and cringe simultaneously. We've come to realize and appreciate the fact that every child is different, learns at their own pace, and is often ready to do different things at radically different times, and that's perfectly fine. Sarang, before he turned three, taught us that.

One day while we were driving along Washington State Route 104, the not quite two-year-old in his car seat behind me looked at the street sign, and said "Rutherfordium" (more like wuthafohdium, as r's are hard). Hold up. What. Just. Happened?! We pull into a parking lot and take out our phones to search Rutherfordium. It's element number 104. How did this happen? We parents glanced at one another,

neither of us having any idea how our toddler knew
what Rutherfordium was, let alone to correlate it to
the state route number. When we got back home,
we were in for a surprise. That afternoon, Sarang
had eaten on a placemat with a supergraphic of the
periodic table. Over the course of that lunch, he had
memorized the table, or perhaps taken a mental
photo, and not only was it embedded in his brain,
but he was also able to make the connection that we
were on Route 104, and pronounce the word as well
as he could in the moment, with his toddler voice.

In the days that followed, we experimented with all
sorts of things, and concluded that he has
something vaguely resembling a photographic
memory, or at the very least picks up information
very quickly, visually and orally, an ability both of us
were fortunate to have growing up as well. Over the
next few months, we did all sorts of fun projects with
him, and he absorbed the information incredibly
quickly. By seven, he was finishing elementary
school curricula in several subjects, and was even

studying middle and high school materials in others, which continues today.

Truth be told, the point here is not about him, exactly. The key takeaway is that we were surprised by our kid, but rather than blow it off as a one off, or push him towards the "norm", we took the time to assess, listen, and experiment with him to see what he was ready for, then provide him with those challenges, regardless of what any external entity, "expert" or otherwise, might say.

A few weeks after the Rutherfordium revelation, Siva gave his notice to leave the job he had loved since he was nineteen, without any hesitation or regret. Siva had poured his heart and soul into teaching high school math at one of the finest schools in the world for a decade, but his heart was at home with our boy, whom he had decided to homeschool. We'd figure out the money side. It had to be done. Anytime the discrepancy between social and intellectual strengths is too vast, schooling is a challenge, whether public, private, or otherwise, and we knew that, having experienced it ourselves to some degree growing up. So, Siva started a small educational consultancy, and has worked with numerous people and learning institutions across the world from pre-K to post graduate, in advancing STEAM (science, technology, engineering, arts, mathematics) education. Aarti carefully selected professional roles that offered her a flexible schedule that would allow her to be home in the late afternoon, to enable Siva to work in the evenings. We were ready to make adjustments to our lifestyle so that we could thoughtfully homeschool Sarang.

One day when Siva was teaching some calculus students, Sarang came in and overheard a bit of the lesson. He recognized a lot of things. He knew all the arithmetic, had some sense of the coordinate axes and ordered pairs, had heard the words slope and area, and had done some basic computations around such things. On that day, at dinner, he asked Siva: "Can you teach me calculus?" What a lovely question to hear from your seven-year-old. Could he? Yes. Should he? Maybe. Would he? Probably not now, but eventually. When he was ready. At this point, you've read enough about our philosophy of parenting and teaching around child-led learning that we're sure you know we didn't dismiss this question with a simple no. We instead talked about what foundations were really needed to get to a place where he could deeply understand calculus and be able to meaningfully apply it. He had the arithmetic down. He had the spatial reasoning down. He had the number sense down. What he didn't have, yet, was some algebraic and geometric foundations needed to fully appreciate the beauty of calculus. So that's what we did. That day we began our study of algebra, with simple, thoughtful questions that grew into more challenging ones, until he was solving algebraic equations fluidly. Now you may be asking two years later if he knows calculus. Not really. Interests change, and cycle. Lately, we've taken deep dives into numerous other areas that have proven to be tremendously fruitful. That said, on the math side, he's still building those strong algebraic and geometric skills, so he's nearly ready to learn calculus!

Before switching gears to Vivaan, let's talk about challenges. Sarang was reading independently before he turned three. He was doing middle school work by the time he was eight. That's not normal, but then again, no child truly is in the sense that there's no actual theoretical average that everyone converges to. Every child is unique, with their own set of exciting strengths and challenges. Many of Sarang's "age-based" challenges came physically and emotionally. Swimming was a tremendous fear. Biking was a Sisyphean challenge, despite his mastery of scootering. Going out of his comfort zone and engaging with those around him whom he was less familiar with, especially without Mom or Dad nearby, was a challenge. These were challenges we overcame together, but perhaps not exactly at the "age-appropriate" or "typical" time. In fact, Vivaan entering the game helped that process tremendously.

Vivaan was not reading at three. He did not appear to have a photographic memory or perfect pitch or "crazy" math skills or some of the other outlying traits Sarang presented at that early age. Vivaan was a happy, sharp kid, who was all about helping others. An empath to the core. Kind, nurturing, loving, and social to a tee. Us parents could best be described as ambiverts. We can be social in small group settings just fine, and in groups centered around activities within our comfort zones, but we're not necessarily that comfortable at those big parties and large get-togethers with mostly strangers. Sarang is an introvert. Vivaan is an extrovert. At least thus far. They're also brothers, and thus complement and help one another out brilliantly. Vivaan at three was adventurous. He loved jumping in the water, climbing trees, riding his balance bike, and more. We always had the band-aids at the ready with this guy. Now you may be wondering how we knew what to expect, given our wildly different experience with Sarang. We didn't. That's it. That said, we acknowledged that we didn't, did our very best to never compare the two boys to one another, but rather to themselves, embody a child-led growth mindset every step of the way, and empower each of them as best as we could, running with whatever interested them and helping them overcome whatever felt challenging to them.

You may recall our discussion a while back about reading *Harry Potter* as a family, as well as our mentioning their love for Pokémon. These two things were in many ways the motivation needed for Vivaan to want to learn to read at four. He saw us and his brother reading, and the stories that came out were so thrilling. He started with smaller words here and there, and gradually grew to sentences and more. We got simple Pokémon stories and phonetics books that he could read independently to build his confidence. We got dinosaur books so he could read stats and pour over data about those creatures he loves, much like his brother did once upon a time. He's still not what we'd call a fluent reader, but he's getting there, and he's doing great. He's also not quite five at the time of this writing. The point here is that there needs to be some intrinsic motivation for a child to really gravitate toward something. Vivaan was ready to learn reading at a different time than Sarang. It was later. He was motivated by the recognition that books provided incredible stories he could learn from, and information about areas that interested him. Vivaan was ready to swim and bike and even play chess tournaments at a different time than Sarang. It was earlier. He was adventurous and loved to try new things. Great. Let's facilitate that. As for math? Well, Vivaan loves numbers too, and is doing just fine with his addition, and extending that to subtraction and multiplication. Are we rushing it? No. We'll go when he's ready. Let him take the lead.

What's the Cost?

Overcoming your inner doubt when someone comments negatively about your child's readiness. Learning to be poised and confident in your approach despite a nagging friend or family member who has no qualms about comparing your kid to another during a gathering. Focusing on the positives and strengths is hard. We're programmed to do differently. That said, as parents, it's critical that we model that positive outlook for our kids as we assess their readiness, especially in our messaging to them, and ideally embody that when evaluating ourselves too, as they're watching our every move. Another "cost" is that you really need to check yourself more. When you see the neighbor's kid or a cousin doing amazing in something, 100% give the compliment, and ideally reach the point where you genuinely mean it. Don't turn it around on your own kid with "Do better like they are." You want your kid to be the best they can be. You can recognize some element of that potential in another child that you want your child to be motivated to pursue. That's all great. Just be careful as to how you craft that messaging. Stick with the positive. Highlight what it takes to reach that level of readiness and help them get there. Avoid negativity.

Aarti and Siva's Reflections

The biggest takeaway for us is that assessing readiness needs to be led by the child. Having benchmarks and guides and parenting books and a doctor's advice and whatnot is fine. They're advisory. They're guidelines. They're indicative of a theoretical "normal" child. In practice, there is no child that fits that profile perfectly. Moreover, there is no child like your child. Every child is unique and the sooner we adults realize that, the better off we'll be. Comparison doesn't help anything. As humans, we have a way of glossing over strengths and highlighting faults. It's a sad reality that's never really left our species as we've evolved over time. If we as parents focus primarily on the faults of our children, how will they view themselves? I'd rather they be confident, kind, caring individuals who acknowledge their strengths and are aware of their challenges, and are willing and empowered to work to overcome those barriers. There's no reason to feel defeated about them.

Kids need encouragement. Kids need to feel like they're doing great and you know what? They are. We may not personally know your kids, but we can guarantee you that they're doing great. How do we know? Think about where they were two years ago. Where are they now? Have they grown? Physically? Mentally? Emotionally? Pretty sure the answer is yes to at least one of those questions, and most likely all of them. Moreover, kids know when you're disappointed, and that can really hurt their psyche. You should be their biggest cheerleader. You can push them. You can discipline them. You can parent with whatever style you feel is best for them, but at the end of the day, you are their biggest motivator. If you feel the need to compare, compare them to where they were. If you feel the need for them to hit a certain benchmark or check a certain box, empower them to be able to do so. Clearly scaffold a path for them. Be their wayfinder. Please let them take the lead though. Where you can. How you can. It'll make a world of difference in your parenting, and for your kids.

Vivaan's Reflection

I love to swim. I love to jump in the water. Slide in the water. Crawl stroke in the water. Play in the water. My mom doesn't. My brother doesn't really. My dad doesn't much but he and my granddad can come in the pool and help me, especially if it's deep. I loved making friends at my swim class. I even taught some chess. We played lots of fun games, in the water and out. I even did a waterslide, several times. I was really scared of it at first, but my family encouraged me, even though they were scared too, and I did it, and I loved it. Right now I'm starting to read on my own. There are some books I can read by myself! Other books I read lots of the words and my family helps me out. I love reading. It's so fun. I really like the stories in books and they inspire me to make stories of my own! One nice thing about being homeschooled is I can stay home and learn what I want, when I want, how I want and go to different places when I want. Dad and Mom and Sarang can help me too.

Sarang's Reflection

I love homeschooling because I can go at my own pace and run with the things I love to learn. I love learning. Some of my favorite subjects right now are Math, English, Science, Japanese, Geography, Chess, and Music composition and performance. I love learning on my own but also enjoy spending time with the friends I've met through chess and music and my other activities. When people ask me what grade I'm in, I say third since that's where I am by age. In my head I know that I'm really at a whole bunch of different grade levels depending on the subject and what I've learned. I feel really good about how much I know but know that there's a lot more to learn. I'm super excited to learn more! I also get to teach Vivaan which helps me master what I know. He also helps me too with a lot of things, especially facing my fears. In fact, I actually did a swimming jump in in a 10-foot deep end once with his encouragement.

<u>Chapter Eleven</u>
Imagination

Activate Creature Power!

I magination is one of the most incredible aspects of childhood. Creating worlds. Telling stories. Bringing ideas from the mind to reality in creative and exciting ways. Setting off on grand adventures in the comfort of home. It's truly amazing, and sadly something that tends to get lost as we age. This chapter features a collection of several experiences that highlight the power of childhood imagination.

Vivaan loves animals. His favorite show is *Wild Kratts*, and his favorite place to visit is the zoo. He reads about animals, he plays with stuffed animals he calls "stuffies," he designs and builds animals, but most of all, he creates hybrid imagined and real worlds with his animals and goes on adventures with them. *As Wild Kratts* does, he'll activate different "creature powers" and pretend to be a rhino or an eagle or a lion, or whatever his favorite animals of the day are, and act out different attributes of the animals as he explores the world he's imagined. This love of animals and desire to pretend play with them proved to be the primary catalyst for Vivaan in his reading journey, as he exhibited such an enthusiasm for them that he eagerly applied his phonetics to animal reference books and *National Geographic Kids* magazines.

Can we talk a minute about dinosaurs? How is the average toddler far more knowledgeable about dinosaurs than the average adult? You know it's true. Kids have some fascination with dinosaurs it's hard to put our fingers on, but it likely stems from the intrigue of a plethora of creatures with interesting features that are no longer around, leaving a lot to the imagination.

We often visit museums, and many of them have dinosaur bones, fossils, replicas, etc. What's incredible to witness is how well the young mind parses the information and constructs a creative classification system. One day, the boys' uncle and aunt were visiting a dinosaur museum abroad that the kids had never been to before. Uncle sends a text to us with four dino skeleton pics with the caption: "Vivi can you identify???" Vivaan, who is watching a *Wild Kratts* episode on something entirely unrelated, glances at the phone and instantly says "Stegosaurus, t-rex, hadrosaurus, diplodocus." When we text back, Uncle responds "Three out of four, amazing!" We tell Vivaan and he instantly responds "Which one did I get wrong? Was it the purple one I said was a diplodocus?" Uncle texts back that indeed it was. Four-year-old V then proceeds to tell us that he thought that one might be wrong since sauropods share similar skeletal features and there are lots of interesting ones the skeleton could be. Uncle tells us it's a futalognkosaurus. We had never heard of it. Vivaan simply says "Ah that makes sense. I know that one. Similar features," and continues his *Wild Kratts* episode. Ok, hold the phone a sec. Did our four-year-old really identify three out of four poor resolution phone photos perfectly, then have the wherewithal to not only recognize which was wrong, but also highlight why it might be wrong with terms like "sauropod" and "skeletal features"? Ok. Good to know. Look, we may homeschool our boys, but we take no credit for stuff like this. It's all them. We just empower them to roll with their interests, and try to facilitate their learning.

Transitioning away from the animal kingdom, imagination is an integral part of our play time together. As we're scooting or biking around, or kicking a ball, or shooting hoops, or whatever, there's almost always some conversation going on about supply chain. Someone is running a restaurant. Someone is buying groceries for the restaurant. Someone is delivering the items. Someone is ordering. Someone is paying. Someone gives change. Someone leaves a tip. Someone leaves a review. It's amazing. It's life. It's teaching them skills they need later on in their created world with different characters. We even change languages as we dabble in different pretend cuisines. The process becomes second nature. Sometimes we're booking a trip. Maybe on this scooting journey we'll travel to some pretend land. We still need to buy a ticket. We still need to figure out how we're getting there. Lots of realism can be brought into pretend play, in order to teach valuable skills. Sometimes we're also emergency vehicles! Though this particular game can get a bit grim, it's also important. Something (pretend) happens. Ok. What do we need to do. Who do we need to call? Ok you're the fireman. Ok, I'll be the policeman. I'll be the ambulance. Literally any kind of pretend play can be fun, engaging, and rooted in real experiences, which all helps facilitate their learning.

A few years ago, when Sarang was six, we worked to leverage his imagination to improve his writing. He had read some kids' graphic novels and wanted to write his own. After doing his research by reading several more, he decided that his main characters would be brother velociraptors, named Vinnie and Valdez, who'd travel the world. He loved dinosaurs, he loved travelling, and he was developing as a writer, not to mention graphic designer, so why not combine everything, have some fun, and learn?! The title of his graphic novel series was "Vinnie and Valdez's Amazing Adventures." They drove a Ford F-150 SVT Raptor all over the world, in this glorious blend of reality and fiction, and past and present, which comes so naturally to the minds of young kids. Vinnie and Valdez met other region-specific dinosaurs, befriended them, and learned about cultures in different places. Through his imagination and love for research, Sarang was able to create compelling narratives, helping not only his writing, but also his confidence and communication skills.

The following summer, he hung out with one particular friend fairly often. The pair of them would go on creative adventures, and, motivated by his newfound penchant for photography, he decided to create another reality-fiction hybrid series with this friend. They would take fun pictures together in curious places on their adventures in real life, then digitally blend them with fictitious elements and weave them into exciting stories from their imaginations. It was pretty cool that at the tail end of the series, they brought their little siblings, also buddies, into their stories and narratives. So when your kiddos come up with their seemingly wild, incongruous, out of the blue imaginative stories, try your best not to pooh-pooh them. Leverage them.

Encourage them. Motivate them to continue being creative and harnessing that imagination into storytelling, writing, drawing, or just play. If you do this, it'll make a world of difference to their creation of happy childhood memories, as well as to their confidence and learning.

Transitioning away from imaginative play, this innate love of the imaginary in children proved crucial for connections during the pandemic. When the pandemic started and we found ourselves feeling cooped up at home, the kids used Zoom as a portal to the outside world. They especially loved to connect with their grandparents. Every week, they diligently logged into the "Theater," where they imagined the great adventures of two characters that traversed many lands on quests, and took turns with their grandparents to make up elements of the story. Imaginative play was an easy way for them to stay connected with their grandparents while creating funny stories, inside jokes, and treasured memories. To this day, they continue the tradition of the "Theater" as their special way of sharing their lives with their grandparents who live many miles away. Was it the same as being there in person? Perhaps not. Then again, the world of imagination transcends physical and spatial limitations so it was lovely to see it used at a medium to navigate trying times.

Time and understanding. Letting kids revel in their world of pretend requires giving them time to do so, and access to situations where they have a buddy or buddies to pretend play with, even if that's you. As for being the adult in the room, just don't be in these moments. Cede control, cede any delusion of every element of their pretend world making logical sense or following a rational progression. It doesn't matter. Also, please *please* **please** try not to kill their vibe. These years of true imaginative play are so fleeting for most that we'd do well to let kids enjoy them while they last, before the world takes them away. And maybe, just maybe, your kiddo will keep growing that incredible imagination to the point where they're the next great fiction writer, screenwriter, podcaster, video game designer, etc. The possibilities are limitless.

Aarti and Siva's Reflections

We can safely say that imagination and pretend play is an integral part of every child's life, until it's not. We all hear the old adages like "Let them be little" or "Just let them be kids," and many of those are tied to this glorious time of unencumbered imaginative play. The key to facilitating and sustaining this wonderful part of a child's life is to encourage it, empower it, and allow kids to experience it fully, which they'll do naturally given the time and space. It could be solo play, it could be with a sibling or a buddy, or it could be with you, the adults in their life. If and when you do engage in this play, as we hope you do, try your best not to be an adult. Be a kid. Revel in that joy the pretend world brings. Sure, you can bring in some elements of real-world learning, but understand that pretend play itself is powerful learning.

Vivaan's Reflection

Sometimes when you're feeling sad or bored, you can do something you like to do to feel better. I love animals. I have lots of stuffies and I love to play with them. I make zoos, tell stories, go on adventures, and have lots of fun.

Sarang's Reflection

When I was younger, I loved creative play and wrote lots of semi-real fiction stories. Now, I'm more of a non-fiction guy in my writing but I bring in creativity in different ways. In music, I utilize my creativity when I compose, improvise drum fills, add musicality to my piano playing, among other things. In chess, I come up with creative new patterns and tactics. In basketball, I come up with new trick shots to challenge myself. Overall, creative play as a younger kid helped me trust my own creative process, which has helped me a lot as an older kid now.

Chapter Twelve
Perseverance

*When Can We Get Our Next
Thousand-Piece Puzzle?*

We love geography. We love traveling. We love learning about different cultures. We love learning different languages. We love data about populations, areas, demographics and more. We also love flags. At Sarang's three-year-old physical, he had an eye test. As they didn't expect he'd be reading yet, they gave him a test based on "figures". One such figure on the 20/20 line was a flag. It was a curious, rather ambiguous flag featuring a single star and horizontal lines. The person administering the test was confused about why Sarang stopped on that one, rather than just saying flag after identifying everything else correctly. We could tell Sarang was a little confused, bordering on irked, until he whispered "Dad, this is some weird combo of the Togo, Ghana, and Burkina Faso flags!" The test administrator overheard and after the initial shock, interjected that all they were looking for was flag. Oh. Ok.

A few years later, as the world descended into the depths of the Covid-19 pandemic, we were gifted a lovely thousand-piece puzzle featuring all the country flags of the world, along with some other regional flags. Sarang was overjoyed. This gift triggered an obsession with puzzles and supergraphics, as well as the development of new skills like process optimization, perseverance. Each time a puzzle was completed, we'd put a clear glue on it, frame it, and hang it on a wall somewhere in our home. Inevitably the conclusion of each puzzle brought about the question "When can we get our next thousand-piece puzzle?"

As the pandemic progressed, puzzling became our greatest way of passing time and connecting with one another, a beautiful, collaborative mental test filled with artistry and learning. Some thousand-piecers we finished in a day. Others took weeks. It didn't matter the complexity. Whatever puzzle we were working on had its special place on half our dining table, and whenever we walked by or had a free minute, we'd sit down and have some fun. Vivaan would help sort the pieces by color or shape, and piece together elements of the puzzles the rest of us had already sorted, like a particular flag, car, or bird. Sarang would do it all. He was ready. As would we. As parents, it was a fun, delicate balancing act to not do too much, and let the kids take the lead, going at their own pace and persevering through the challenge, but also enjoy family time and help them solve it.

Seeing both kids' joy as they solved little bits of the puzzle each day was beautiful. There was the light at the end of the tunnel, so to speak, as they knew it would eventually be put up somewhere in our house for all to see, and hopefully when they look up at each of these beautiful works of art, they remember the time we spent together puzzling and persevering. Over the course of the pandemic we did thousand-piecers featuring national parks, butterfly migration, totem poles, the tree of life, flags of the world, VW beetles, Mickey Mouse, the periodic table, emojis, trains, birds, the mythical world, plants, animals, families, instruments, and more. Now, years later, we still reminisce when we walk by one in the hall, about the time we spent together doing it: a beautiful time capsule memory and work of art all in one.

LEGO was a natural love following all this puzzling. Like Vivaan does now, Sarang adored building things as a little kid. He'd use Magnatiles, and Lego Duplo, and train kits, and plane kits, and you name it. When Sarang was eight, some of his chess friends invited him to join them in First Lego League, a competition for kids to design intricate worlds out of Lego, following particular themes. Cargo Connect was the theme he worked on. It was amazing. He and his friends would do builds every week, to brainstorm for their innovation project, on how they could improve transportation infrastructure. At the end of each week, the kids were able to see and appreciate the progress they had made, even if it was only a little. They knew carrying the mission through to completion would be a long process, and they were ok with that. They planned and they persevered.

Coding is a beautiful way to build perseverance. Sarang began his coding journey by learning Scratch, a block-based language that allows kids to learn important elements like conditionals, loops, and such, through a user-friendly drag-and-drop interface. Soon that journey led him into game design. Like with Lego League, he would have a vision for what the game would look like and how he wanted it to be played, and from there figure out all the structural elements needed to achieve that vision. It was slow going, with lots of roadblocks. After each hour of coding, he had learned a lot more about what not to do than what to do. But as his toolkit of what not to do grew, so did his success and efficiency on the next iteration. As he improved his fundamentals, the worlds he created became more elaborate, and the programs he designed much more robust. The value in baby steps was clear. I still remember how excited he was when he finally figured out how to create the health meter and point scorer for his character. These are things gamers take for granted, but are fascinating for kids learning to code. To thrive in coding, like with puzzles and

Lego, a growth mindset is key. There are always new and exciting challenges, no matter how good you get. You'll fail, and you'll fail often, and every failure is an opportunity to learn and grow.

Returning to Lego League, once all the builds were done, they had to make their robot, and put their now extensive Scratch coding skills to the test by having their robot perform various missions with their builds. This was even slower going, and completing challenges with time limits in particular required lots of iteration, failure, and patience. They did it though. They persevered. Most notably they had fun in the process. Because they were confident in their abilities, they knew that if they worked hard they'd succeed, even if they had several "failures" along the way. Through the process, they learned to appreciate incremental gains, which are often easy to overlook, and acknowledge that learning what may not work is an important step in learning what will.

Shortly thereafter, Sarang got into Lego architecture. These sets were intricate and had labels like 12+, or even 18+ in some cases, but by now you know how we feel about these purported age limits. He started with the skyline of New York, a place he wanted to visit. Next came London. Then Paris. Soon after, he was gifted the Taj Mahal, a monstrous 2000+ piece set for ages 18+. It had so much nuance, and so many layers and levels. It didn't matter. He was ready. He knew it would take time, but that's fun! Every day he'd do a little bit. When his activities were lighter, he'd do a bit more. Pretty soon it began to take shape. After about a week, he'd done it! He had built his own Taj Mahal.

Patience, commitment, work ethic, and yes, perseverance, aside, a beautiful thing about this whole process was how invested he got in what he was building. Not just the Lego versions, but the real places. For the skylines of New York, London, and Paris, he'd research what all the buildings were. He'd learn about the history of each city, and what there is to see and do. He even did some planning for potential actual visits to the places at some undetermined time in the future. It was beautiful to see him persevere through an experience and travel to an exciting new place, all from the comfort of his bedroom.

One Christmas, the boys' uncle gifted them an indoor, over-the-door basketball hoop. They couldn't wait to assemble it and start playing. Once they had mastered basic shots, they graduated to trick shots, where they would come up with an elaborate sequence of moves to be performed before the shot could be considered valid. The kids spent hours trying to land their trick shot, sometimes needing over a hundred tries. Then they would try another hundred times, or however many they needed to pull off a repeat performance! As they worked hard on perfecting each trick shot, we would point out how they were persevering, and encourage them to apply the same dedication in other facets of their life. We used these moments to remind them that most things require hard work, dedication, and practice. We've seen the same perseverance from them with video games. With no prompting, we've seen them try the same race many times until they perfected every drift, every jump, every shortcut, and conquered the game. We leverage their love for basketball and video games to foster positive habits in other aspects of their lives.

For example, when Sarang initially learned a difficult piano piece, he was so close to giving up, and lamented that he was never going to be able to master the fast passages. At that point, we asked him to reflect on how many hours he had worked on a particular trick shot, or race, before succeeding. He thought about it, then said that he had practiced one race for nearly a month, and had watched several YouTube videos from his favorite gamers to understand all the shortcuts. We naturally extended what he said to piano playing. Mastering the fast passages was the same as mastering a video game – they both required quick fingers, precision, and dexterity. Getting fast didn't happen overnight with a video game, and wouldn't with the piano either. And just as he had learned key skills from others to speed up his video game playing, he had to leverage his teacher's expertise to master the piano techniques needed to be successful. Lastly, he needed to practice the passages relentlessly every day until he was happy with his playing. Once the concept of perseverance clicked in his head, his piano practice has been self-driven, and he has made so much progress in his playing.

What's the Cost?

Time and parental awareness to understand where your children will naturally practice perseverance and where they will not, and to help them apply what works for them in successful situations to areas where they struggle. Building perseverance requires facing an initial failure, additional setbacks, and repeated attempts to overcome them, which takes a lot of time. The good news is you can spend a month on a jigsaw puzzle and it'll never cease to provide fun and challenge! The key is having the perseverance and growth mindset to be ok at the end of the day with having connected only a couple of pieces, knowing you're setting the stage for more the next day.

A crucial idea is that helping kids build perseverance can happen through fun challenges, like puzzles, Lego builds, coding, and even video games. By facilitating them learning this important skill in safe, low-stakes environments, they become more adept at applying it to real life setbacks. They also learn the importance of baby steps and repetition, and gain the ability to recognize the value of knowing what doesn't work in addition to what does. Finally, learning perseverance provides them with perspective in situations of potential disappointment. Every setback is a learning opportunity, and they know they can persevere.

Vivaan's Reflection

When I'm building with my Magnatiles and one piece isn't working, I just take it off and try again with another piece or a different arrangement of the pieces. Sometimes my creations collapse but that's ok. I just make them again even better, maybe with some other stuff, like braces on the outside.

I love building. I love designing. I love creating. When I was little and I was building shapes like truncated icosahedrons and cube octahedrons and whatnot, I used to get a little upset when they broke down. Then I decided to reframe my thinking, enjoy the process of building, and honestly, most of the time after I built whatever I was building, I had fun breaking it down too when I cleaned up! When I made the skylines, I imagined being in the cities. The pieces were very small and sometimes I hurt my fingers trying to connect them at first. Then I got better. Sometimes some structures were really delicate and would break like the Eiffel Tower and London Eye. I didn't get mad though. I built them once and I could build them again, this time faster and more effectively. The Taj Mahal was a challenge y'all. It took several days and each day I only did one to two bags and sometimes it didn't look like a lot was happening. At the end though, everything was there and the whole process felt so worth it. As for coding, I started with Scratch and did lots of fun projects and game design in that language. I then moved to Lua to code in Roblox and plan to move on to JavaScript soon so I can design websites. I love that there's a continuous feedback loop in coding and that I can constantly learn from my mistakes and keep getting better.

<u>Chapter</u>
<u>Thirteen</u>
Inspiration

*We're Brothers. He Inspires
Me and I Inspire Him.*

We all have different strengths. We all face different challenges. If we can use our strengths to overcome our challenges and become our best selves, while simultaneously inspiring others, we've made a positive difference. Perhaps in writing this book, we've shared some inspiration with you. Writing it has certainly helped us codify what we value, and doing so all together as a family has been bonding time we'll cherish forever.

With a little over four years between them, Sarang has always been the primary source of inspiration for Vivaan. Sure, Vivaan's looked up to us too, but we're just not the same as his awesome older brother, who does all the cool things that he wants to be part of, and is so smart and can relate to all the things he's going through, having gone through them himself relatively recently. Sarang's inspiration got Vivaan into chess at two. Sarang's inspiration got Vivaan into piano at four. Sarang's inspiration got Vivaan into drums at four. Sarang's inspiration got Vivaan into singing at four. Sarang's inspiration got Vivaan into his band and gospel choir at five. No doubt elder siblings can often inspire the younger ones. That said, it really is a two-way street.

As a toddler, Sarang was, unequivocally, securely attached to us. He was comfortable with his grandparents and uncle and a few other family members, but broadly speaking he preferred to keep to himself and close family. He didn't crave activities. He didn't crave social interaction. He didn't crave friendships. In fact, when we tried daycare for a short while when he was a toddler, it was a disaster. He's brilliant, in many senses of the word, and much of our job as parents is to facilitate and empower that brilliance. He now has a plethora of activities he's thriving in, and is a confident leader in group settings. So what changed? Simple. Vivaan entered his life. You see, when Sarang was three, he asked us for a sibling: someone he could bond with, play with, inspire, and teach. Once we realized our rather avant-garde paradigm of homeschooling, with one of us working during the day and the other working in the evening, was sustainable after beta-testing it for a year, we took him up on his request.

When Vivaan came into the picture, everything changed for Sarang. On the one hand, he got his wish. He had a sibling. A little bro. A mini-me of sorts to inspire, protect, and bond with. A lifelong buddy who shares his genes, passions, and intelligence. While he got all that, the brotherly bond quickly became so much more. In fairness, initially it was a bit tough for him, as his then two favorite people in the world—us—had our attention divided and frankly, probably more focused on the baby, though we tried our best to find balance. As Vivaan grew, however, a switch clicked for Sarang. He needed to show this little kid how to learn. How to act. How to play. How to live. How to be. And that's exactly what he did. But what he may not have anticipated was the profound impact Vivaan would have on him. Vivaan, no doubt securely attached to all three of us, was nonetheless very comfortable with all family, and friends as well. He was great at reading faces, and if he saw that you were comfortable with him, he'd happily be comfortable with you too. As Sarang witnessed this bubbly little bundle of joy bouncing from person to person and conversing with everyone he could in his sweet little voice, he began to do the same. The inspiration was flowing the other way.

Fast-forward a few years and Vivaan is like a little fish. He loves the water. He jumps in happily, dunks his head, and is eager to learn floating and swimming. The water had always been dangerous territory for Sarang, who preferred to err on the side of caution. Sure we pushed him to learn swimming as a younger kid, but he never really took to it and had a serious fear around "head bobs," aka sticking his head underwater, and outright refused to jump in the water. One summer, when Vivaan was four and Sarang was eight, Vivaan was taking his swim class. The local swim club had two-week small group sessions that met for a half hour daily. Vivaan loved them. Sarang loved watching Vivaan loving them, from the sidelines, while playing speed chess with his dad and whoever else might want to try to challenge him. About six weeks into the summer, however, something clicked in his mind. Hmmm. If my four-year-old brother loves swimming class so much, sticks his head underwater, and jumps in the pool so happily, maybe I can too? He even tried the water slide! I was always too scared to do those things but if he can do it, why not me too? On registration day for the fourth two-week session of the summer, Sarang quietly asked "Do you think I could give this a try again too?" Surprised, excited, and wanting to capitalize on this moment, we asked the staff members in charge if there was a class for him, a slightly older kid who wanted to give swimming a try again. They said of course. They knew him as the huge chess guy and awesome big brother who as a little kid used to go in the pool before the pandemic.

That next session was amazing. We were initially concerned it would be a repeat of the struggles Sarang faced in the pool as a toddler, in the before-times. Our fears were unfounded, however: everything was different. Vivaan had entered the picture, and he was inspiring Sarang just as Sarang had inspired Vivaan time and time again. That very first day, as they went to their respective classes, it was Vivaan telling Sarang "You got this bro," before they hugged and walked into the pool together.

Fortunately, Sarang had an inspirational teacher who bonded with him over their shared love of Mario Kart. When Sarang was asked to jump in, he refused. His teacher didn't push. When he was asked to do a head bob, he paused, psyched himself up a little bit, saw his little brother across the pool bobbing like a fish giving him a smile and a thumbs up, and you know what Sarang did? A head bob. And another one. And another one. It may have a taken a pandemic spent away from the water, an inspirational little brother, and a new and improved outlook on life to do it, but it happened, and it was awesome. In the days that followed, Sarang followed Vivaan's lead and refamiliarized himself with floating and the basics of swimming, gained more and more comfort sticking his head under water, and started doing it with increased frequency. He still wouldn't jump in, though.

Leading up to the final class of the term, so much progress had been made by both boys, which we were of course thrilled about. In the car ride on for the final day, Vivaan was encouraging Sarang to just try jumping in. At least once. If only to prove to himself that he could do it. During this time, Sarang was actively coaching up Vivaan at chess, and Vivaan had started doing tournaments despite some trepidation about being by far the youngest player, and some challenges around learning how to lose and such, all of which Sarang was helping him with beautifully. As we were nearing the club, both boys were teeming with nervous energy and excitement for their last class for the summer and over the thought of Sarang jumping in for the first time, something his coach had also gently encouraged him to try on the final day. And then, in a moment of deep introspection, Vivaan said something that none of us will ever forget: **"We're brothers. He inspires me and I inspire him."**

The rest, as they say, is history. Sarang took this messaging to heart. He jumped in during that final class. He jumped in from the deep end. He popped right back up as one would expect him to. He was fine. Did he like it? Probably not. Will he do it again? Who knows. But in that moment, after years of fearing the water, after a couple weeks of overcoming much of that fear, he finally conquered it altogether, thanks in large part to the inspiration of his little brother, jumped into that pool, his full body immersed in the water, and popped back up. Just fine. After getting congratulated by his coach, do you know what he did? He went across the pool to his little brother and gave him a hug. That's what it's all about y'all. That's what it's all about.

What's the Cost?

Nothing. Literally nothing. You have everything to gain by both drawing inspiration from others and providing inspiration to them. Don't know how? Just be yourself. We are all "geniuses" in some way or another. We need to believe that. YOU are amazing. We all have our strengths. We all face our challenges. We get over our challenges by drawing on our strengths and inspiration. By exercising our strengths we inspire others to get over their challenges. It's a beautiful way to build one another up and grow together.

What can we say. It warms our hearts. We are blessed. We have the privilege of calling two lovely humans our children, whom we intentionally do our best to empower as much as we possibly can. How do we facilitate an environment of mutual inspiration? We try to highlight strengths all the time. We try to lift our kids up whenever we can. We try to help them find ways to reflect on and acknowledge their challenges, and think of creative ways to overcome them. We try to help them find inspiration around them, and do their best to be inspirations for others in turn. A former student and dear friend once told us that we're the only couple they'd ever met who are both geniuses, and also genuinely believe and articulate regularly that the other is the smarter one and that we are much more successful and empowered because of our partner. You know that old thing folks say about don't do as I do, do as I say? That's rubbish and frankly doesn't work. We've found a more effective approach is to be your authentic self, see the best in those around you, and when you see something awesome in someone, say it. Build people up. Inspire them. Hopefully, when they are inspired by you, they'll reciprocate, and you'll be inspired by them. When you see a friend or family member facing a challenge, especially one you've overcome yourself, offer to lend a hand, and share your experiences. Let them take you up on it when they're ready. Always remember: inspiration is a two-way street and we're all the better for it.

Vivaan's Reflection

Sometimes when things are hard to do or you're afraid to try something, you need some inspiration to help push you through. Sarang has helped me so much in finding my voice and sing in my three different groups. He also helps me with my drumming and piano playing. He also helps me with chess. Most of all, he has helped me by being such a good person and role model. In the first several weeks of swim class, whenever Sarang was looking and waving, I would jump in and head bob. I loved doing it and I knew it could help him try it someday. It was so fun when he was in the pool with me. At the end of every session, we held hands and swam in a circle singing a motorboat song and that was so fun. I'm glad I can help my brother just like he helps me.

Sarang's Reflection

What do you want me to talk about? It feels so nice to hear that I'm making a positive impact on my brother's life by inspiring him. I can actually dunk myself in the water pretty consistently now! I was always very afraid of going down and not coming back up. I had read about drowning and was afraid I might die. By seeing Vivaan do it, over and over, having so much fun, it helped me face my fear. I'm an introvert. That hasn't changed. Even so, I love my circle of friends from music and chess and sports, and I love playing with them and being a leader in my different activities. Vivaan helped me with that too. He's naturally a really friendly guy and watching him make friends has helped me do the same.

Conclusion

Dear Friends,

First and foremost, we want to thank you for taking the time to read our book, share in our stories, and hopefully get a glimpse into a rather wonderful lifestyle centered around intentional parenting and child-led learning. We're hopeful that you enjoyed the ride and found some ideas that might resonate with you, challenge you, or motivate you to try something new. We acknowledge and appreciate that every family is built differently with unique strengths and challenges. We are also firm believers in a growth mindset and continually like to hone our own practices in the hopes of improving every day.

As we went through the ideation, writing, editing, and publishing processes together as a family, the power of reflection really stood out. Could we have got this book out to you sooner? Perhaps. Then again, if we did, we wouldn't have had the time to really reflect on every step of the process, enjoy that family bonding time around these memorable experiences and stories, and crystallize the takeaways that matter most to us and hopefully made an impact on you as well.

We chose curiosity, planning, exposure, connection, awareness, resilience, privilege, confidence, goals, readiness, imagination, perseverance, and inspiration as the themes to highlight our family stories around child-led learning and intentional parenting. Which resonated with you? What would you add? Anything you'd remove? We're completely serious when we say we want to keep the conversation going, hear your ideas, and share more of ours. Please follow sankrithibooks.com for continued updates and don't hesitate to message us personally at sankrithibooks@gmail.com.

Love,

The Sankrithi Family

About the Authors

The Sankrithi Family is a unique family of Indian descent living in the United States. This is their debut co-authored book in the collective voice of life partners Siva #DadLife and Aarti #MomLife, along with their two boys Sarang #BigBro and Vivaan #LilBro, aged nine and five at the time of writing. Siva retired from teaching at a prestigious independent school in Seattle to homeschool and work as an educational consultant. Aarti has worked in engineering, supply chain, and finance. Bridging the best of East and West, the pair challenge and empower one another on their intentional parenting path. Sarang and Vivaan lead the way on their own remarkable educational journeys, filled with music, chess, travel, and more.

Made in the USA
Middletown, DE
24 September 2023

38842522R00130